Evolving BEYOND Thought:

Updating Your Brain's Software

GARY WEBER PH.D.

© 2017 Gary Weber Ph.D.
All rights reserved.

ISBN: 197972377X
ISBN 13: 9781979723770

Library of Congress Control Number: 2017917837
CreateSpace Independent Publishing Platform
North Charleston, South Carolina

Dedicated to Ramana Maharshi who found me lost and wandering in a dark forest, taught me what inquiry, love, and surrender were and brought nobody home…

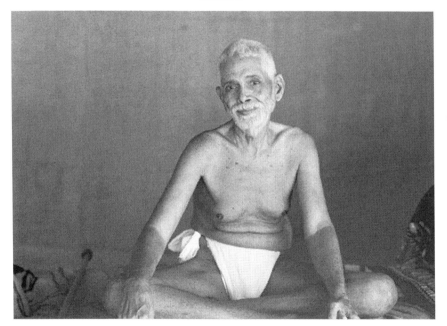

Reviewers' Comments

Rich Doyle

Author of "Darwin's Pharmacy: Sex, Plants and the Evolution of the Noosphere", "Wetwares: Experiments in Post Vital Living", "On Beyond Living", and "Into the Stillness: Dialogues on Awakening Beyond Thought" (with Gary Weber).

What a treasure! Imagine browsing a shelf of obscure and esoteric wisdom books and stumbling upon this potent software manual for debugging your own mind. In Evolving Beyond Thought, Gary Weber offers engaging diagnostics and nondual practices of self repair for a noggin full of thought and its longtime companion, suffering.

Weber offers a practical and no nonsense overview of your buggy old operating system infected with the malware of "I", and then he shares the countermeasures: Focused attention on selections from the Ribhu Gita kindle a glow of awareness beyond the "I", while digital correspondence with a thoughtful practitioner, Oskar, points the way to an everyday life - yours - illuminated by nonduality.

This book spills over with diverse recipes for hacking our minds beyond the "I" – a radiant liberation from long suffering mind. Read it, evolve beyond thought, and be free.

Chris Guimond

Hi Gary

I've spent many hours studying your manuscript. I did a first quick read to get an overall sense of the structure, (which I like very much), then reading and re-reading to try to look at it objectively, for its 'usefulness' for a sincere seeker. I also tried to look at this book from the vantage point of having no 'pre-requisites', like familiarity with your other books and videos - not easy! Also appreciate the sense of humour in the table of contents for the first section!

I love all the four sections, but particularly the Ribhu Gita section, and the fact that you have posed thoughtful questions paired with verses and your very helpful commentary. It was a revelation for me to learn how much the "I am this body" idea is at the root of SRIN! Several weeks ago, had just added working with 'I am not the body' and discovering the felt truth of that statement was like a key turning in a lock.

I find a lot here to be of great usefulness, truly an invaluable resource, and have underlined and highlighted many gems for my own benefit. Also really appreciated the whole section on free will and dialogues with Oskar. The section on free will cleared up some lingering questions and confusion.

Definitely this book is not going to be of interest to the masses! But for those that find their way to this book, it could prove to be an invaluable companion, much like I Am That.

I had previously read through much of the blog posts and dialogues with Oskar, and feel they totally belong in this book.

Hi Gary

...Returning home yesterday, my husband said he had something extraordinary to share with me, saying 'I discovered while you were away, i am not my body!' He read the first half of your manuscript, and had been investigating this idea.

Both of us are seeing astonishing changes in each other over the last several months; much softening, openness, presence, kindness, humility, love. Incredibly radical changes in our relationship. Love is the greatest healer.

Hi Gary,

...Something else I am noticing this time around, it feels like something truly marvelous has happened to my brain, like I have taken an extraordinary leap in my learning ability - beyond the improved capacity for sustained attention.

I've noticed steady improvements, in the last couple years, but it's a surprisingly big change that has happened since the first week of September. Wouldn't have thought this possible. Marcel has also remarked that he can see big changes in my cognitive abilities. Have you, or your students experienced this?

In fact, Marcel is so impressed with the changes he sees, he has begun reading your book Dancing Beyond Thought, and is going through your YouTube videos with great interest!

Robert Wright

Author of "Why Buddhism Is True: The Science and Philosophy of Meditation and Enlightenment", "The Evolution of God", "NonZero: The Logic of Human Destiny", "The Moral Animal"

In Evolving Beyond Thought, Gary Weber makes the case for transcending ordinary consciousness, with its delusional self-absorption, and explores underappreciated ancient texts that illuminate the path he has followed to this end. Weber's deeply personal book gives us reason to believe that 'non-dual' awareness, even if rarely attained, is attainable and infinitely repays the effort involved in attaining it.

TABLE OF CONTENTS

INTRODUCTION

No matter where you go or what you do, you live your entire life within the confines of your head.

Terry Josephenson (1)

Our current Homo-sapiens operating system (HS-OS "I") is clearly not up to today's massively-interconnected and highly-complex institutions, governments, religions, technologies, and resource constraints. It is obvious that we are confronted with highly-dysfunctional societies that have great inequities in distribution of critical resources for survival, have inefficient and corrupt organizations, and unsustainable population growth that is causing great damage to the environment.

i believe we are at a "tipping point". If we don't soon make fundamental changes in how we interact and function, the issues described above, largely resulting from our egoic, "I"-based current operating system, could well destroy us. The change from the belief that the "I" is a constant, fixed, real, entity to understanding that it is just an "ad hoc", haphazardly-assembled, mental construct, needs to be as fundamental, obvious and clear as "the earth is round".

So how do we go about updating our brain's software?

The first section of the book focuses on a systematic approach to working directly on the problems with the current operating system (OS) and its programs. The process begins by removing our current, outdated OS "I" (focused on the "I") and evaluating the success of the removal. An updated OS "mini-me" (less focused on the "I") is then installed from several trusted and reliable sources. Next, the most problematic programs are removed or significantly modified.

The second section provides a powerful tool to support this process, seemingly exactly tailored to it, the Ribhu Gita. Sections devoted to "Am 'I' these thoughts?", "What is this mind?", "Am 'I' this body?", "What problems arise from this belief (that 'I' am this body)?", "What am 'I'?" and then "What are the benefits of this knowledge of the Self?". This text was a/the favorite of my main teacher, Ramana Maharshi, and aligns perfectly with his "direct path" of self-inquiry for nondual awakening. It is powerful to read and to chant.

The third section demonstrates that this self-inquiry and letting-go-of-attachments process works in the "real" world with a "real" job. Through dialogue with someone going through the process over a significant length of time it shows how the process actually unfolds.

The fourth section focuses on the most problematic, strongly-held, and tenacious of the programs in the current OS "I", the issues of "free will", control and predetermination. This is the stronghold of the egoic/I structure. Selected comments, questions and answers from blogposts on the issue address resistances, objections, and problems that arise.

Throughout the book, to bring emphasis to the distortions incorporated into our language supporting the importance of the ego/I, no personal pronouns will be capitalized if they start a sentence, and throughout "I" is replaced with "i" unless the egoic "I" illusion is being discussed. The only exception is when "She" is used for "God" or "Universal Consciousness".

Anglicized Sanskrit terms are spelled as they are pronounced, not how they are commonly used in English, as in replacing "asana" with "aasana". How words sound does matter.

Updating Your Brain's Software

Removing OS "I"

How do we remove, or dramatically downsize and re-assign our "I" to develop a fundamental change in our OS? What, if any, "I" functions are useful and can be retained?

Our OS "I" developed about 75,000 years ago. Our predecessors broke off from the chimpanzees about 6,000,000 years ago. Homo sapiens manifested about 200,000 to 300,000 years ago, so the "subject – doing – object" based, symbolic logic and languaging with its "I" is a recent innovation.

After this split from the chimpanzees, brain size increased threefold and evolved many organizational and neural modifications before OS "I" could emerge. There was a pressing need to coordinate and organize increasingly larger groups as our population grew, we moved out of caves and began "hunting and gathering" and competing with similar species.

Symbolic logic and its languaging was a revolutionary approach. It enabled us, uniquely as a species, to coordinate large numbers of ourselves and our resources to solve a wide range of complex tasks in different and changing environments. With it, we were able to eliminate the four competing Homo hominina (1) sub-species, develop agriculture and grow our numbers exponentially.

Today's complex, highly-interconnected, resource-constrained and crowded world has demonstrated the many limitations of the OS "I" in this very different environment. Attempting to cope, we have developed a persistent, self-referential internal narrative (SRIN) desperately trying to control, direct, forecast and manage situations which are far beyond its capabilities.

At an individual level, this consumes huge amounts of energy, wastes most conscious bandwidth with poor signal/noise ratios, and increases problematic negative, emotionally-charged energies. This leads to depression, anxiety, disease, worries, craving, attachment, suffering, etc. At a global level, there is endless conflict from the division into my country, my religion, my belief, my race, my money, etc. leading to wars, terrorism, inequity, and exploitation.

Recognition that SRIN was THE source of my unhappiness manifested in grad school while walking to campus working on a Ph.D. in materials science. An epiphany arose that it was just "not acceptable" to have this never-ending cacophony; there had to be a better way. Having no idea if it was even possible, i set out to see if/how SRIN could be eliminated.

Serendipitously reading the first line of a Zen poem, "everything" changed dramatically. A state manifested for 30 to 45 minutes, of great presence, clarity, energy and most importantly, no thoughts. It WAS possible to stop SRIN. As this was a "Zen" poem, i set off to find some Zen folk to discover just how to do it.

Having a strongly empirical bias, this investigation was conducted empirically, not intellectually or philosophically. It would be validated through personal experience, not millennia-old speculation. Some experimental "design parameters" manifested:

a) Only contemporary sources with videos, photographs, audio recordings, and/or direct transcripts of information would be used.

b) Living sources, preferably fluent in English, were to be seen personally or validated by highly-credible sources.

c) Ongoing feedback on progress was provided continuously from the SRIN, itself. If SRIN was still there, then more work was needed.

d) The process must retain or enhance functional "real world" performance.

e) Happiness would increase, and suffering, stress and anxiety would decrease.

f) The result must be an ongoing, natural, change in "life" or state, not just passing experiences.

g) It would be scientifically verifiable and secular.

After much searching, the "removal tools" that manifested that satisfied these criteria, and that worked, were from the self-inquiry approach of the 20th-century sage Ramana Maharshi. (2) This approach also appeared in a shorter form in the Zen literature as developed by the 14th century Japanese Zen master Bassui Tokushoo. (3)

As demonstration of the validity of this choice and focus, Ramana Maharshi said in response to a question regarding the world's problems in the 1940s: (4)

*2e: There are great men, public workers, who cannot solve the
       problem of the misery of the world.*

Ramana: *They are ego-centered; hence their inability. If they remained
          in the Self, they would be different.*

Many different meditation approaches were also investigated, including mantra, Transcendental Meditation and mindfulness/shikantaza/Soto Zen but
they did not deconstruct the "I". This was subsequently validated in the
experienced-meditator research at Yale University in direct comparison of
self-inquiry with Vipassana/Theravada/mindfulness meditators as described
in the article, "The Neuroscience of Suffering – And Its End". (5)

Direct empirical approaches manifested to understand thoughts, how they
were constructed, whether they were continuous or intermittent, energetic or
not, linked or "stand alone", how the "I" was constructed, etc.

These involved putting thoughts of different types, like a) past/now/future,
or b) I/me/my and no I/me/my, into different "buckets" over a few minutes
to undersand their nature. A straight line was drawn every time a thought
stream changed subject metter to see how erratic they were. Exercises were
done to see if thoughts could be predicted, or whether they were "thought up"
or just manifested "all by themselves".

Self-inquiry is simply, persistently and curiously investigating "Where am I?", "Who
hears?", "When am I?", "What has this thought?", etc. Most sessions begin with
classical Zen breath counting from 1 to 10 or 10 to 1, or breath awareness followed
with self-inquiry. With continued practice, the changing manifestation illusory
nature, and haphazard and accidental origins of the "I" are investigated thoroughly,
and its questionable value revealed. Ultimately it weakens and falls away.

Comparing the processing capability of the conscious and the sub/un/non-
consciuos processing powers of the brain can be hepful in letting go of the "I".
A useful metaphor is that of a rider and an elephant.

The "rider" is the "I" with its "conscious", on-line processor that generates the SRIN, and that uses symbolic, subject-doing-object logic to talk to itself about itself. The "elephant" is the massively interconnected, "sub/un/non-conscious" off-line processof or 800 billion neurons which does all of the heavy lifting as well as almost everything else.

Neuroscience has found that the rider can only handle 7 +/- 2 pieces of data at a time, across virtually all languages and can only solve one problem at a time. Its processor runs at **40 to 60 bits/second**..(6)

The "elephant" has something like 100 trillion synaptic interconnections, according to the latest research, for handling and storing information and operates and something like **25,000,000 bits/second**, depending on applications and assumptions (7) There are good evolutionarily logical reasons for this arrangement.

The total computing power of the brain is determined by how many discrete areas are operating at the same time. Obviously, seeing, hearing, smelling, tasting and touching can go on with talking, texting (not so much), walking, driving, digesting food, breathing, pumping of blood, hauling away waste, sending energy bearing glucose to and oxygen to working areas, problem-solving, etc.

Estimates for this massively-parallel processing put the entire brain's capacity as high as 320 billion bits/sec for the entire brain. Ninety-nine percent of which "we", the "riders" are , thankfully, unable to perceive or interfere with. If the "rider", with its limited processing power, were to try to "fix it", it would likely be a disaster.

The "bottom line" is that the "rider" has 1/500,000th of the capability of the "elephant". Why then does anyone listen to it? It's just a confused press secretary, disconnected CEO, apologist, critic, judge, jury, etc., contributing little beyond endless talking to itself, about itself, with itself.

SUCCESS

After many, many hours of meditation and yoga, the SRIN stopped and there was a deep powerful, natural, effortless Stillness and Presence that has continued for 95+% of the time since manifesting in 1998.

The meditation and yoga leading up to that stretched over 25 years, 2 hours a day, every day, no matter where i was in the world. Practice varied as different approaches from many traditions were tried. There were also weekend and week-long retreats.

Now spontaneous practices manifest for hours a day, every day. As a famous Zen quote says, this understanding is "capable of endless enlargement". (1)

Practice was not always even and uneventful. There was no attempt to re-member experiences as the consistent advice from the teachings was to ignore them as they can become a trap, which i found to be the case.

This realization was passed by my two very different Rinzai Zen masters, Toni Packer (2) and Roshi Eido Tai Shimano (3). In Rinzai Zen, authorized masters rigorously evaluate, one-on-one, the progress of students, with a series of questions, and then evaluate them based on the answers and the way in which they are answered.

SRIN can manifest when my blood sugar gets very low (hypoglycemia) or when the body is very tired. Most early mornings, some items from the day before manifest in a "should this be sent to long term storage or discarded" manner. If no interest is shown in it, it just fades away.

Simultaneously, a loss of self-referential fears and desires, and a significant increase in functional capability manifested.

What also fell away, which was totally unexpected, was the loss of any sense of "free will" or control, simply because there was no one there to have it. Despite previous expectations of chaos and turmoil, it was obvious that "my life" was running better without "me" in it. "Something" was arranging everything with incredible skill and knowledge that far surpassed any capability that could have been previously imagined. Surrender into this "something" followed with the discovery that the more i surrendered the more i was held. When complete surrendered manifested, there was total support in a powerful, yet compassionate way.

The stopping of SRIN is what Ramana Maharshi said would happen. Many ancient texts, contemporary teachers, and spiritual traditions focused on "enlightenment", define "having no thoughts" as their goal, recognizing that the OS "I" is the root of our problems. (4)

The desirability of having "no thoughts" was researched in "Just Think: The Challenges of the Disengaged Mind", by Wilson, et al. University students and middle-aged townspeople were seated in a chair in a large room alone, with nothing to distract them from themselves for 10 to 15 minutes. The consistent result was that folk really didn't want to "be alone with their thoughts". They would even give themselves a painful electric shock rather than be alone with their SRIN. (5)

As Blaise Pascal said, "All of humanity's problems stem from man's inability to sit quietly in a room alone". (6) This is the reason for our many, many diversions...anything but being alone with our thoughts.

There is also much validation emerging from cognitive neuroscience on the negative impacts of SRIN. Studies demonstrates that wandering minds produce premature aging (7) and unhappiness (8).

When SRIN stopped, there was no cognitive neuroscience, so scientific validation had to wait until the last 10 - 15 years. Real-time fMRI technology can now ascertain whether someone stopped their "blah, blah"/SRIN and shut down their default mode network naturally without effort, or if ongoing tasking is required.

This natural, no efforts, "no thoughts" state was validated in the fMRI experienced meditator work at Yale University in 2011 discussed earlier.

INSTALL A NEW OS MINI-ME

With the validated uninstallation of the OS "I", the question was "What, if anything, would be installed to replace it?". As the great Stillness and Presence was so different from "business as usual", there was a strong feeling that some coherent, generally-accepted "logic" was required to put the intellectual brain at ease in this new situation.

When asked how one functions in this state, Toni Packer said "Read Nisarga-datta's 'I Am That'", which was found to be exactly what was being experienced. (1) Other key OS mini-me elements came from Ramana Maharshi's teachings. Reading, learning, memorizing and chanting Nirvana Shatakam and Ramana's Upadesa Saram and recommended verses from the Bhagavad Gita in Sanskrit laid down the basic logic for OS mini-me. (2)(3)

Success in removal of OS "I" and uploading of OS mini-me was verified by the continued absence of SRIN. Problem solving and planning tasks were enhanced when the problematic SRIN-causing "I" elements were removed. This was a huge (and welcome) surprise.

As cognitive neuroscience manifested, it was discovered that different neural circuits were used for these different functions. Three discrete neural networks - Default Mode, Tasking, and Control - were identified as responsible for different functions.

The Default Mode Network is where "self-referential" functions are processed and where the sense of an "I" passing through time and an "I" different from other objects is created. This is where the problematic "blah, blah", talking to itself about itself, originates.

The Tasking Network is where non-self-referential problem solving, planning, analysis, etc. are conducted. This is not problematic and the processing and "thoughts" have a different "energy" from those in the Default Mode

Network. The brain can learn to differentiate between these and process them differently. The Control Network has the function of switching between these two networks.

This is discussed in detail in "The default network and self-generated thought: component processes, dynamic control, and clinical relevance" by Andrews-Hannah, et al. (4)

As with all new software there are programs for implementation, procedures, learning problems, etc. The programs for the identification, removal and upgrading of the OS "I" software are described in "Happiness Beyond Thought: A Practical Guide to Awakening" which also includes the Nirvana Shatakam, Upadesa Saram and Bhagavad Gita programs. The Bhagavad Gita program is explained in detail in "Dancing Beyond Thought: Bhagavad Gita Verses and Dialogues on Awakening". (5) (6)

DISCONTINUE SUPPORT FOR THE CONFIRMATION BIAS PROGRAM.

Confirmation bias is *"to search for, interpret, favor, and recall information in a way that confirms one's preexisting beliefs or hypotheses, while giving disproportionately less consideration to alternative possibilities."* (1)

This program was evolutionarily-useful as it facilitated focusing on information that enhanced the understanding on some important subject, like where the lions were, and rejected extraneous, distracting information, like where the giraffes were. "Lion" information was gathered, remembered and interpreted in a biased way, like what our cave or hunter-gatherer group had experienced in coping with lions and where and when they were most likely to be found.

However, although our "lions" are now political, religious, economic, institutional, etc., that same confirmation bias program is still running. This program is so strong that even "unbiased" evidence is skewed to align with our existing biases. Evidence contrary to our biases is heavily discounted or "massaged" to align with our biases. Our selection of sources for our evidence is heavily focused on those that support our biases.

In one fMRI study, when participants were shown contradictory statements by their favored political candidate, some of which were irrational or hypocritical, the emotional centers in the brain were strongly activated as they worked to *actively reduce* the divergence of the information from their beliefs. (2)

Confirmation bias also exists in meditation research. The Johns Hopkins research by Goyal, et al. in "Meditation programs for psychological stress and well-being; a systematic review and meta- analysis" published in the Journal of the American Medical Association found that only 10 of the best 47 mindfulness meditation studies were unbiased.

This study also found insufficient evidence of any effect of mindfulness meditation programs on positive mood, attention, substance use, eating habits, sleep, and weight and no evidence that these meditation programs were better than any active treatment (drugs, exercise, and other behavioral therapies), despite many mindfulness studies that had found just the opposite results. (3)

"Fake news" works because of our confirmation bias program. The CEO of Disinfomedia, Jestin Coler, said that he employed "from 20 to 25 writers at a time and made $10,000 to $30,000 monthly from advertisements" creating fake news. (4)(5) Teenagers in Veles, Macedonia were found to be getting rich by generating "fake news". (6) To check your confirmation basis, use a news service where you can change your news sources and their weightings, and see how your feelings change.

An interesting demonstration of confirmation basis comes from the cartoon video, "You're not going to believe what I'm going to tell you". (7)

This exercise is about George Washington, the first President of the United States who had *wooden teeth* as he lost most of his teeth in his twenties.

Reading this, how does this make you feel? Take a minute and see how/what you feel about the first President of the United States having wooden teeth... good, bad or indifferent.

OK, now how do you feel when you learn that the National Museum of Dentistry found that George Washington's wooden teeth *were replaced with gold, lead, hippopotamus or elephant ivory, horse and donkey teeth?* Another source included cow teeth, and silver and copper alloys. (8) (9) Take a minute and feel that.

Finally, it was revealed from two other sources that George Washington had many teeth in his dentures *from the slaves on his plantation.* (10) (11) Take a minute. Now how do you feel about George Washington?

These stories are all true, but did you see how much your feelings changed towards George Washington as the stories changed? That's confirmation bias.

UNINSTALL RECIPROCAL ALTRUISM PROGRAM AND UPGRADE TO OPEN SOURCE.

Compassion is basically our response to the suffering of others that motivates a desire to help them.

However, "love" is much more complicated, as we all know, arguably so multi-faceted as to be a nearly meaningless term. As Wikipedia cautions, *"This diversity of uses and meanings combined with the complexity of the feelings involved makes love unusually difficult to consistently define, compared to other emotional states."* (1)

A famous Christian saying is "A new command I give you: Love one another. As I have loved you, so you must love one another." Recognizing this ambiguity, a new term arose, "agape", from Homer and the Greek translation of the Bible, which translates as "the highest form of love, charity". (2)

Whatever term is used, responding to the needs of others is a heavily evolutionarily-encoded behavior for strengthening the bonds and structure of our group. It is a key element in our evolutionarily-successful strategies of co-operation, task-sharing, and hierarchical organization. A recent article "How homo sapiens became the ultimate invasive species" said that we "conquered" the planet and became "the ultimate invasive species" with the weapon of co-operation. (3)

To reinforce these behaviors, a supportive reward system using dopamine and oxytocin evolved to give "rewards" to ensure that we do it... we feel "good" when we are "compassionate" and "co-operate".

As His Holiness, the Dalai Lama, said:

*"Human beings may naturally be selfish, but they are also naturally compassionate, science shows. Helping someone else does make a person feel good – but that is **a wise kind of selfish**."*

"By nature, every human being loves oneself," the Dalai Lama said. *"But by helping another, you are building your own happy future. We should be wise-selfish rather than foolish-selfish."* (4)

Evolutionary psychologists have a more cynical view of this "helping others". They call it "reciprocal altruism", defined as *"a behavior whereby an organism acts in a manner that temporarily reduces its fitness while increasing another organism's fitness, with the expectation that the other organism will act in a similar manner at a later time."* (5)

This boils down to "i'll do something to help you, but i expect to get something in return later", with the implication that "if you don't do something for me later, i won't help you again".

Reciprocal altruism was introduced by Robert Trivers and criteria for such behaviors were developed subsequently by Christopher Stevens:

1. the behavior must "cost" the donor

2. the recipient must get more benefit than non-recipients

3. the behavior must not depend on receiving immediate benefit

4. these conditions apply to both individuals involved

For reciprocal altruism to "work" there must be a mechanism for detecting 'cheaters' who don't repay and many opportunities to exchange aid.

Other species evolved their own "reciprocal altruism" systems, including parasite removal in fish, bird calls when seeing predators, and primate grooming. However, the human reciprocal altruism system is described as "sensitive and unstable" so it needs dopamine-reinforced pleasure to reinforce it. (6) (7)

Religions created "reciprocity" for self-ish, compassionate acts by promising significant *future* benefits or punishments in an "afterlife". Concepts of good or bad karma, virtue or sin, etc., are to lead to better or worse rebirths, nicer heaven or worse hell, longer or shorter time in-between, etc., but there's no real evidence that it happens.

With all of this, including neurochemically induced pleasure, humans still have a hard time being compassionate. Have we evolved to be impossibly "selfish"?

Despite millennia of practice, it is hard to see where the religious-based, reward or punish approach has worked. A secular, non-selfish approach is needed. The Dalai Lama agrees, "With more education, religion might disappear in the next 1,000 years", and has proposed a solution with secular ethics in his "Beyond Religion: Ethics for a Whole World". (8)

Watching the "market-based" operation of reciprocal altruism, it clearly compromises actions. What is given is what is imagined, with own conditioning and biases, that other folk "should have", which is often *not* what the other really needs.

With the decrease in the strength of the "I" concept as described earlier, what naturally occurs is a decreased sense of there being anyone needing something in return for an action including the neurochemically-enhanced pleasure. There is also no requirement that whatever manifests in meeting another has to match "my" expectations or conditioning. A total openness is available for whatever might arise out of the stillness and presence. Only by meeting others in this way can we be truly useful in supporting them with what they really need. The video "Upgrading Your Mental Operating System" discusses this. (9)

Use malware removal tools on the attachments programs.

Removing attachments is an important aspect to couple with self-inquiry in unwinding the "I" which is their root, and reducing the suffering they cause. As the Buddha said in his Second Noble Truth, "The origin of suffering is attachment." and in his Third Noble Truth "The cessation of suffering is attainable." (1)

Adi Shankara, an 8th CE (most likely) Advaita icon, generated Nirvaana Shatakam, a comprehensive check list of attachments which is very useful for deeply, and actively, exploring all of our attachments, element by element. Having chanted it thousands of times, Nirvana Shatakam is the gift that keeps on giving. (2) (3) (4)

Despite the initial resistance to learning Sanskrit and to chanting, works chanted in their original manifestation generate a deeper level of understanding of what the writer encoded than does reading, particularly of translated texts. This encoding conveys the original writer's knowledge and understanding like a great painter, sculptor, or musician putting into their creations what can be directly experienced centuries later.

With continued practice, as elements in Nirvana Shatakam like "mother", "family", "good deeds", "pride" and "death" are chanted and focused upon, the underlying network(s) of neural real estate holding the stories, fears, anxieties, beliefs, traumas, etc. for that element will manifest. When these manifest, they are investigated with the "malware programs" of the Byron Katie and Sedona approaches and are "let go of". They then disappear or are greatly weakened. (5) (6)

Working with these amazingly-effective, cognitive-behavior-therapy based protocols as described in "Letting go of your attachments to awaken...why/how/when" and "Surrendering the 'I', letting go of suffering" and the video

"Letting go of suffering and attachments", can dramatically reduce and potentially eliminate problematic attachments. (7)(8)(9)

The success of removing attachments can be easily determined with repetitions of Nirvana Shatakam and changes in the SRIN generated by them.

UNINSTALL THE "FREE WILL, I'M IN CONTROL" PROGRAM.

As it is evolutionarily-encoded, complete with a universally-experienced "feel" of having it, "free will" must have been "a great idea at the time", but it isn't true, scientifically or logically. As it also forms a keystone of most religions, judicial systems, institutional structures, marketing approaches, etc., it is deeply-held, widely-reinforced and strongly-defended. However, in that regard it's a lot like "the earth is flat", or "the earth is the center of the Universe"...universally perceived and "obvious", but wrong.

For decades, i KNEW that i had free will, and consciously chose and was re-sponsible for everything that happened. Resultant successes and failures were "mine" with the accompanying praise and blame. However, when the "I" fell away, there was simply no one there to have a will to exercise. Amazingly, "my life" was better without "me" in it. It was obvious that choices and respon-sibility were misconceptions. This has been one of the most liberating and surprisingly empowering changes in perspective in this Dance.

What do we mean by "free will"? With a Ph.D. in neuroscience and a Stanford degree, Sam Harris' "Lying" and "Free Will" offer a clear perspective on these difficult topics. The popular conception of free will is that a) we could have behaved differently than we did, and b) we are the conscious source of our thoughts and actions in the present. Are these assumptions correct? (1)(2)

If we watch carefully, acts that we *believe* we decide to do, actually arise spontaneously, without our conscious involvement. Their origin cannot be seen with our conscious minds, nor can subsequent decisions to perform them. The reason and justification for having done them is created by the conscious brain after the event. For 99+% of the day, actions occur "all by themselves", effortlessly, perfectly.

The current neuroscience strongly supports this. David Eagleman, a leading neuroscientist, said in a recent PBS series, "Our conscious minds play a much smaller role in our lives than we once imagined. Everything from what we do, to who we are, is orchestrated by the unconscious brain...The human brain is nature's perplexing masterpiece." (3)

Do you pre-think your next thought, or does it just manifest without conscious knowledge or approval? When you write (or text) something, do you "think it up" before it appears, or does it just appear from "nowhere"?

Watching the apparent choosing of which green tea to drink, the hand reaches for the Jasmine rather than Zen or Ginger, but there is no conscious "reason" for the action. Jasmine just "feels" right. If subsequently asked for the "reason", what emerges is, "i had Zen this morning, and was almost out of Ginger, so Jasmine was the obvious choice". This response was completely "made up" by the "I" to make it appear like the choice was conscious and logical.

The cognitive neuroscience demonstrating that free will is an illusion is compelling. Benjamin Libet, et al.'s, ground-breaking, paradigm-shattering, research in *Brain* in 1983; "*Time of Conscious Intention To Act in Relation to Onset of Cerebral Activity: The Unconscious Initiation of a Freely Voluntary Act*", demonstrated that the motor cortex initiates actions well before the conscious "I" is even told about it, and well in advance of the actions being performed. (4)

If we aren't even aware when, or what, action is initiated, how can we be in control and have free will?

Libet's work, which received the inaugural "Virtual Nobel Prize in Psychology", caused a firestorm of hostile reactions. Nonetheless, with more sophisticated technology and experimental designs, his work still stands.

Libet himself tried to "save" free will by arguing that when the brain was informed that the action was in process, it could have been "consciously" stopped. However, the decision to stop the action, or not, would arise just as the initial action did, without our knowledge or conscious control.

A conclusive, widely-publicized, demonstration of "no free will" was conducted by J. D. Haynes in "Decoding and Predicting Intentions". Haynes demonstrated that it was possible to reliably predict intentions, with an fMRI, 7 to 10 seconds before the decision was actually made. (5)

Also, Fried, et al. in "Internally Generated Preactivation of Single Neurons in Human Medial Frontal Cortex Predicts Volition" demonstrated that recordings from only 256 neurons could predict with 80% accuracy a decision to move 0.7 seconds before one became aware of it. The "recruitment" of neurons (assembling a project team) occurred 1.5 seconds before subjects reported making the decision to move, validating Libet's results. (6)

The brain determines what you will do, well before you are aware that you will do it. Events are no more initiated "consciously" than are the beating of the heart or the digesting of food. What will the next mental state, thought, decision, or action be? It just happens, "all by itself".

This "no free will" and "determined" phenomena is not confined to Homo sapiens, but is universal. As Albert Einstein said:

"Everything is determined, the beginning as well as the end, by forces over which we have no control. It is determined for the insect, as well as for the star. Human beings, vegetables, or cosmic dust, we all dance to a mysterious tune, intoned in the distance by an invisible piper." (7)

To actually have "free will" and "control", Sam Harris says "You would need to be aware of all the factors that determine your thoughts and actions, and you would need to have complete control over those factors...What would influence the influences?...You are not controlling the storm and you are not lost in it. You are the storm." (8)

A typical question is "If there is no free will, why should I do anything?"

Ramana Maharshi answered:

The feeling 'I work' is a hindrance. Ask yourself 'Who works?'. Then the work will not bind you, it will go on automatically. Make no effort either to work or to renounce; it is your effort which is the bondage.

What is destined to happen will happen. If you are destined not to work, work cannot be had even if you hunt for it. If you are destined to work, you will not be able to avoid it and you will be forced to engage yourself in it.

So, leave it to the higher power; you cannot renounce or retain as you choose. (9)

What about the retributive justice system if there is no free will, no personal responsibility? If "what we are" is determined by genetics, parents, where/when we were born, religion, friends, etc. which were not of our choosing, and we don't know what our actions will be, how do we deal with criminal acts, and everyday relationships?

These arguments are already manifesting in the criminal legal system. Farahany showed in "Neuroscience and behavioral genetics in US criminal law: an empirical analysis" that instances in which judges cited neuroscience evidence in their opinions increased from 112 in 2007 to over 1500 in 2011. (10)

Integrating this scientifically-demonstrated fact into our religions, institutions, government, legal system, health care, etc. is going to be disruptive. Some scientists and ethicists have argued that it would be better "if we just don't tell them about it", which is like continuing to tell folk that the earth is flat, or the center of the universe in the face of compelling science to the contrary.

The Catholic Church's punishment in 1616 of Galileo for asserting that the earth was not the center of the universe, was reconsidered, and after a 13 year investigation in 1992 was *moving towards* the compelling science as described in "After 350 Years, Vatican Says Galileo Was Right: It Moves". However, it was still being debated in 2008. (11)(12)

"There's no 'free will'...accept it, attack it, hide it or ignore it?" gives the recent neuroscience and desperate approaches to "save it". (13)

See for yourself. Watch any day, and see if anything comes out exactly as you expected. Yes, you get to the Starbucks, but did you know what would happen getting there, or what happened when you got there, or who would be there? Look at what's happened "in the world" in the last 6 months...were you in control of any of that?

So, let's update our operating system and clean-up our outdated programs and save our species for those who will follow after us, and for our own uncaused happiness and liberation from suffering.

Additional information is available at www.happiness-beyond-thought.com including a listing of books, presentations, articles, interviews, blog, MP3 links, youTube channel, soundcloud channel and a comprehensive bio.

A Powerful Tool For Updating Your Brain's Software – The Ribhu Gita

Introduction

The Ribhu Gita is one of the most powerful, and yet, least well known, of the major Advaitic texts, even in India. Arguably, it was the favorite book of the most revered sage of the 20th century, Ramana Maharshi. It was one of the first books that Ramana Maharshi read after reaching Tiruvannamalai following his awakening at the age of 16, where he would spend over 50 years on, in and around, his beloved sacred mountain, Arunachala.

Advaita, or nonduality, is the philosophical, experiential, and scientific understanding of non-separation and intrinsic Oneness. It is literally "not two" or "one undivided without a second". There have been tomes written on it, but it is directly experienced as "All is One" - no separation from others, and "now, now, now" - no past or future. Although virtually every religious tradition has a "mystical" sect that has arisen within/from it that has this perspective, nonduality is inherently "anti-religious". A religion has a "God" that is separate and different from "me". In nonduality, "you" are "God" but so is everyone, and everything else.

Ramana described his state at the time of reaching Tiruvannamalai:

"I did not know that there was an Essence or Impersonal Real underlying everything and that God and I were both identical with it. Later, at Tiruvannamalai, as I listened to the Ribhu Gita and other sacred books, I learnt all this and found that they were analyzing and naming what I had felt intuitively without analysis or name." (1)

In the early days, Ramana and his devotees would chant the Ribhu Gita together virtually every night, in Tamil, the predominant regional language, with each one reading a verse in their turn.

As one of his early devotees, Sampurnamma, recalled:

"One day he gave me a copy of Ribhu Gita and asked me to study it. I was not at all anxious to pore over a difficult text good only for learned pundits, and asked to be excused, saying that I did not understand a single word of it". Ramana replied, "It does not matter that you don't understand. Still it will be of great benefit to you." (2)

The Ribhu Gita is from the Shivarahasya Purana which has 12 parts, and about 100,000 verses in Sanskrit. Some sources claim it is 7000 years old, which is likely metaphorical, but possible. The Ribhu Gita is the Sixth amsa/part and is regarded as its very "heart". It has about 2,200 stanzas/verses that capture the dialogue on the Self and Brahman by two sages, Ribhu and Nidagha on the slopes of Mt. Kedara in the Himalayas. (3)(4)

The dialogues between Ribhu and Nidagha are also captured in the Tejobindu Upanishad of Krishna Yajurveda, Mahopanishad of Sama Veda, Annapoorno-panisha of Atharva Veda and Varahopanish of Krishna Yajurveda. (5)

Working carefully with the Ribhu Gita, reading, learning, and then chanting it, you can feel it working deeply within.

The 32 verses that are included in this compilation were selected to deal with several key issues that arise in the path to nondual awakening:

a) "Am I these thoughts? What is this mind?" - Five verses from the chapter on "Topic of the Brahman-Bliss"

b) "Am I this body? What problems arise from this belief?" - Seventeen verses from the chapter on "Determination of The Phenomenal World Being the Void and Nonexistence of All"

c) "What am I?" - Eight verses from the chapter on "Description of the Bliss of the Self".

d) "What are the benefits of knowledge of the Self?" - Two verses from the chapter on "Instruction in Brahman-Conviction" (6)

Two earlier books were titled, "Happiness Beyond Thought: A Practical Guide for Awakening" and "Dancing Beyond Thought: Bhagavad Gita Verses and Dialogues on Awakening". As many major spiritual teachers have pointed out, the goal of meditation and yoga is to arrive at a persistent state, not just an experience that is fondly remembered, "beyond thought".

This "no thoughts" goal is expounded by Ramana Maharshi, Nisargadatta Maharaj, Dogen Zenji, Patanjali's Yoga Sutras, The Bhagavad Gita, The King James Version of the Christian Bible, Bhante Gunuratana, The Katha Upanishad, Dzogchen Master Chokyi Nyima Rinpoche, the Vigyana Bhairava Tanga of Kashmir Shaivism, the Tao Te Ching, Padrino Paulo Roberto - founder of the Santo Daime syncretic religion, Hui Neng in the Platform Sutra, the Yoga Vasishta Maharamayana of Valmiki, the Hatha Yoga Pradipika, Paramahansa Yogananda, Swami Sivananda, Alan Watts and J. Krishnamurti, to name just a few. (7)

It is important to realize that "no thoughts" is the goal in meditation, and of nonduality, simply because if there are "*self*-referential internal narrative thoughts",

the SRIN discussed earlier, remaining, then there is clearly a
maining as well and more work to be done. SRIN is an imme
free, constantly running indicator of one's progress towards nondual awakening.

It is important to recognize that there are different "types" of thoughts manifesting through different neural networks, for different purposes which can
be managed differently.

The "blah, blah", self-referential, problematic, emotionally-charged thoughts
(SRIN) originate in the Default Mode Network. (8) Non-problematic planning, problem-solving and analysis thoughts originate in the Tasking Network.
There is a separate Control network which manages the switching between these
two networks. (9)

The types of thoughts referred to in the Ribhu Gita are the "blah, blah" problematic ones, which constitute over 95% of most folks' interior mental state and
number something like 70,000 per day. These generate our anxiety, neuro-
ses, fear and depression. Research studies have demonstrated that this internal
narrative while sitting alone, without any entertainment, for 12 to 15 minutes
causes most folk such discomfort that they will give themselves a painful electri-
cal shock to be distracted from it. (10)(11)

Fortunately, the brain can differentiate between these two types of thoughts, and
problematic ones can be dealt with through self-inquiry meditation and letting-go
exercises. The problem-solving, planning thoughts can then function more efficiently and effectively as the bandwidth and energy consumption of the "blah,
blah" thoughts are gone and the signal/noise ratio has been improved dramatically.

The order of the verses was selected by the order in which they typically arise
in a nondual awakening practice.

First, there is disengagement from the thoughts and then understanding
that the mind is only a collection of thoughts and the cause of many great

misconceptions. Next comes the pervasive belief that we are these bodies, which lies at the root of the ego/I concept.

The emphasis on "Am I this body?" reflects the importance of this topic. The fundamental change, the turning of the page from illusion to clarity and understanding in my process of nondual awakening, occurred after many, many hours of self-inquiry and yoga while working with "I am not this body" and "Am I this body?" in an inverted posture/asana in a yoga vinyasa/flow.

Only then do the verses on "The Bliss of the Self" arrive with the refrain "anandam param manam", or "Bliss is the primary measure".

The concluding verses summarize the benefits of knowledge of the Self as the underlying reality of Universal Consciousness. As the Bhagavad Gita says in Chapter 13, Verse 27, "He who sees the Self, residing equally in all beings – the imperishable among the perishable – sees clearly." (12)

These 32 verses are easy to learn and chant and provide all of the important concepts. IME, to really "get" their full meaning requires learning and chanting it. Key phrases and repetition deepen their impact while providing sufficient differentiation for the brain to link them and place them in the right order. These teachings, like an impressionist painting, great poetry or music, can then reach across hundreds or thousands of years and communicate the transcendent message from its creators.

Brahman, Aatman, Shiva, Universal Consciousness/She, etc. will all be represented by "Self" which is distinguished from the "self" of the ordinary ego/I of self-referential thought. All are pointing at the transcendent "something" which cannot be accurately described, only experienced, of which we are all part, which pervades everything.

During my journey, as letting go/surrender occurred, to great surprise, the more i let go, the more i was held by some loving, compassionate energy, which clearly felt "feminine", unlike the masculine "Gods" in many religions. With total letting go, there was total support, in accord with a famous Bhagavad Gita verse, Ch. 9, Verse 22, and all my needs are met and protected. That is why "She/Her" is often used when referring to "the field of Universal Consciousness".

ARE MY THOUGHTS USEFUL? HOW DO THEY "BEHAVE"?

cittam	eva	mahaa	doshaM	cittam	eva	hi	baalakaH
Thought	alone	great	folly	thought	alone	is	small boy

cittam	eva	maha	atma	ayaM	cittam	eva	maha	anasat
Thought	alone	great	soul	this	thought	alone	great	unreality

Thought alone is the great folly. Thought alone is the small boy. Thought alone is this great man. Thought alone is the great unreality.

The opening verse goes to the heart of the issue with thoughts and the problems they create in our lives. Since "folly" comes from the French word "folie" meaning "madness, stupidity", it gives some indication of just how thoughts mislead us as to where we should place our attention and efforts. (1)

Similarly with the metaphor of the "small boy". As we watch small boys, they are often darting from this, to that, to that… Thoughts are like that, darting from place to place, never remaining on a subject, emotion, or story for long before moving on to another diversion. This is a frantic search for something, anything, to fill up that deep emptiness we feel, that great "lack" gnawing at us continuously.

The "great man", also translated as "great soul", is somewhat confusing. However, it is referring to what "great (wo)men" imagine they are, enhanced, expanded and reinforced by thought. If those distorted thoughts were not there, then the (wo)man might find (her)himself dancing through life with Presence, Awareness and true compassion for whatever arose, moment by moment by moment.

Thoughts create their own "world" that exists only in that consciousness, an ongoing parallel universe, often with no relation to what is manifesting in the "real" world. There is not even awareness of the body-brain's adroitly navigating its way, "all by itself" through life.

The latest neuroscience demonstrates that over 99% of our actions are controlled by our "non/sub/un-conscious" off-line brain, the "elephant", whose actions the "conscious" on-line brain, the "rider", cannot even perceive, let alone control. (2)

Evolutionary development created a "rider", a user interface functioning as press secretary, judge, jury, critic, apologist, etc. that talks to itself about itself, all day. It can only handle 7 +/- 2 pieces of data at a time, functions at 40 to 60 bits/second and can solve only one problem at a time.

The "elephant" parts of the brain have over 100 trillion synaptic interconnections for data storage, information handling and manipulation, and processes information in a massively-parallel way. Processing speeds are roughly 25,000,000 bits/sec for an aggregate rate of something like 360,000,000,000 bits/sec. Virtually all bodily functioning, and all complex, important problem solving, planning, analysis, choosing, etc. is done "off line".

Excellent research has demonstrated how, where and when the brain does this solving of complex problems requiring "1,2,3, a,b,c, 4, 5, 6" type insights, "off line" in the "elephant", and then informs the "on line" conscious "rider", that the problem has been solved so that it can claim and proudly announce victory. (3) (4)

JUST HOW UNREAL ARE MY THOUGHTS?

cittam	eva	hi	mithya	atma	cittaM	shasha	vishanavat
Thought	alone	is	illusory	self	thought is	hare's	horn

cittam	naasti	sadaa	satyaM	cittaM	vandhyaa	kumaaravat
Thought	is not	is ever	true	thought	like the son	barren woman

Thought alone is the illusory self. Thought is like the hare's horn. Thought is never true. Thought is like the son of a barren woman.

That statement that "thought alone" is the "illusory" self (distinguished from the Self) is perhaps a surprising conclusion. Watching thoughts, the ego/I/self is always there, imbedded in virtually every conscious thought. Deconstructing this ego/I/self and its attachments, it becomes clear that all that is, is Self.

Two classical metaphors of unreality - the son of a barren woman and the horns of a rabbit/hare - point out that like them, self-referential thought is unreal and inherently false. Watching carefully, see if any self-referential thoughts accurately predict the reality of what happens. Do the imagined scenarios occur as expected, or were many unexpected? Did serendipitous events manifest that weren't, and couldn't have been, "thought of"?

As discussed earlier, that is why the state of "no (self-referential) thoughts", or SRIN, is the most widely accepted measure of the nondual awakening process. It is a free, installed, and continuously available monitor of the continued existence of the ego/I.

The challenge of reaching "no thoughts" is captured by Ramana Maharshi:

> "If one wants to abide in the thought-free state, a struggle is inevitable. One must fight one's way through before regaining one's original

primal state. If one succeeds in the fight and reaches the goal, the enemy, namely the thoughts, will all subside in the Self and disappear entirely." (1)

"Dhyana means fight. As soon as you begin meditation other thoughts will crowd together, gather force and try to sink the single thought to which you try to hold... This is the battle royal always taking place in meditation. One wants to rid oneself of misery. It requires peace of mind, which means absence of perturbation owing to all kinds of thoughts." (2)

The Bhagavad Gita gives a very simple and straightforward approach to getting to this "no thoughts" state in Chapter VI, Verse 25:

shanaiH	hanaiH	uparamet	buddhyaa		dhrti		grhiitayaa
slowly	slowly	withdraw	with the intellect		steadiness		endowed

aatma	saMstham	manaH	krtvaa	na	kincit	api	cintayet
in the Self	fixed	mind	making	not	anything	whatsoever	think

One should gradually, gradually, attain stillness, with an intellect endowed with steadiness. Fixing the mind in the Self, (with the idea "The Self alone is all; there is nothing apart from It") one should not think of anything whatsoever.

Shankara, the great codifier of Advaita Vedanta/nonduality, has said about this verse, "This is the highest instruction about Yoga." It is about as compact and "tight" as one could imagine for a description of the process used to accomplish nondual absorption and abiding in stillness without thoughts. (3)

GARY WEBER PH.D.

WHAT AM I? WHAT IS THE SELF? DO MY THOUGHTS HAVE VALUE?

cittam	shuunyaM	na	sandehaH	brahma	eva	sakalaM	jagat
Thought	emptiness	no	doubt	Self	alone	whole	world

aham eva	hi	caitanyaM	aham eva	hi	nir	gunam
I am alone	verily	consciousness	I am alone	verily	without	gunas/attributes

Thought is emptiness — there is no doubt about this. Self, alone, is the whole world. Verily, I am, alone, consciousness. I am, alone, without attributes.

Another interpretation of the last line would be "I am consciousness, I am without attributes."

This is a powerful summary verse, encapsulating three different structures of presenting the text as well as three very distinct and important messages.

The first message, "Thought is emptiness/void" is a classical message mirroring the Heart Suutra, the best-known and most popular Mahaayaana Buddhist scripture, in which a key passage is typically interpreted as:

"Form is no other than shuunyata, shuunyata is no other than form. Form is exactly shuunyata, shuunyata is exactly form". (1)

"Form does not differ from the void, and the void does not differ from form. Form is void and void is form." (2)

(Note that throughout, when Sanskrit words are used, they will be spelled as they sound, so that they can be correctly pronounced, not as how they are popularly anglicized, i.e. "suutra" vs "sutra".)

34

This has always struck me as a misleading translation, as it is not what is actually experienced when one reaches the state of persistent nonduality. This may be because the authors, or the translators, were not practitioners or did not themselves reach the state of persistent nonduality, but instead stopped only part way along that path.

Folk who reach the state of persistent nonduality find it is nothing like a "void" with its negative and nihilistic connotations.

I have used "full emptiness" and "empty fullness" in place of "Void", to describe what is actually observed. As described later in the Ribhu Gita, "anandam param manam", or "bliss is the primary measure" of one's realization…a far cry from the "Void" and "Dark Night of the Soul" (DNoS) of Christianity and Mahaayaana Buddhism.

This "Void" translation has, IME, led to many unfortunate, intense experiences of "Dark Nights of the Soul" (DNoS) suffering for Buddhists, Christians, and others conditioned to believe that great suffering is a prerequisite for enlightenment. There is no such expectation or description in Advaita/nonduality, hence it rarely manifests. Nondual awakening is not without challenges, fears and difficult periods, but they are not the disabling dysfunctionality of DNoS found in mindfulness practices.

Much of this difference is due to the ongoing use of self-inquiry in nonduality as the process unfolds, which deconstructs the ego/I which is at the root of DNoS. Increasingly, mindfulness teachers, for this reason, are adding self-inquiry to their repertoire. The blogpost "Dark Night of the Soul?...why/why/what to do?" discusses this in detail. (3)

The second message of "Self alone is the whole world" is a recurrent theme, and again mirrors the experience of nonduality and transcendent mystical states of "All is One". Cognitive neuroscience demonstrates that the perception we have of ourselves "different from others/objects" is constructed by a sub-network in the Default Mode Network.

Similarly, the sense of "ourselves passing through time with a past and future" is created by a sub-network in the Default Mode Network. If this is deactivated by nondual meditation, psychedelics, or other approaches for reaching a "transcendent" state, then the experience of living "now, now, now" manifests. (4)

The third message is one which we see throughout the Ribhu Gita, of "I am, alone, consciousness. I am without attributes."

The "I am, alone, consciousness" experience is a fundamental one in nondual awakening. Through diligent practice of self-inquiry and "letting-go of attachments", the ego/"I" is deconstructed and what is revealed is blissful consciousness without objects, doing, subjects, etc.

The powerful Nirvana Shatakam, which is chanted in the "Shut Up and Chant" video and included in "Happiness Beyond Thought", goes through a systematic unfolding and negation of the attachments and obstacles in the nondual awakening process. The refrain at the end of each verse starts with "I am blissful consciousness. I am blissful consciousness." (5)

The "gunas" or "attributes" are important concepts in philosophical schools across Samkhya and Hinduism. The most useful definition is "quality, attribute, and property" and the three gunas are – *sattva* (knowledge, happiness), *rajas* (passion, attachment, desire) and *tamas* (inertia, laziness, ignorance, lack of discrimination) which "bind the immutable embodied being to the body". (6)

Everyone has these gunas in different degrees at different times, and is subject to, and embodied by, their constant change and dance...unless they can transcend them and "awaken". The entire 14th verse of the Bhagavad Gita is dedicated to transcending these gunas.

As described in XIV, 5, such a person is called a "*guna-atiitaH*", or one who has transcended – "*atiitaH*"- the gunas. Verse XIV, 21, asks "By what signs is one known who has gone beyond these three qualities (gunas)? What is his behavior, and how does he transcend these three qualities?". The answer is given in the following verse, XIV, 22:

prakaasham	*ca*	*pravrittiM*	*ca*	*moham*	*eva*	*ca*	*paandava*
illumination	and	activity	and	delusion	even	and	Arjuna

na	*dveshti*	*sampravrttaani*	*na*	*nivrttaani*	*kaankshati*
not	dislike them	when appear	nor	when disappear	long for them

When illumination, activity and delusion appear, he does not dislike them, nor does he long for them when they disappear.

"Prakaasham" is associated with the sattva guna; "pravrittim" with the rajas guna, and "moham" with the tamas guna. If one transcends them all, even as they do their inevitable dance, one does not dislike any particular one of them when they arise, nor does (s)he long for one which has gone away. (7)

This verse if often misinterpreted. Much focus is placed on reaching a sattvic state so that one is not buffeted by the dance of rajas/activity and tamas/laziness/inertia. However, this is not the ultimate goal. Even sattva, the illumination arising from knowledge, can lead to attachment. Complete liberation goes beyond attachment to even the sattvic state.

HOW DO BONDAGE, SIN AND SAMSARA ARISE?

mana	*eva*	*hi*	*saMsaaraM*	*mana*	*eva*	*hi*	*mandalam*
mind	alone	is	samsaara	mind	alone	is	the circle

mana	*eva*	*hi*	*bandhatvaM*	*mana*	*eva*	*hi*	*paatakam*
mind	alone	is	bondage	mind	alone	is	sin

Mind, indeed, is the worldly existence. Mind, indeed, is the mandala.
Mind, indeed, is bondage. Mind, indeed, is sin.

"Samsaara" is rooted in the term Saṃsṛi which means "to go round, revolve, pass through a succession of states, moving in a circuit". This has expanded to a "passage through successive states of mundane existence", a circuit of living where one repeats previous states, from one body to another, a worldly life of constant change that is rebirth, growth, decay and re-death. This is contrasted with the concept of moksha, also known as *mukti, nirvana, nibbana* or *kaivalya*, which refers to liberation from this cycle of aimless wandering. (1)

Samsaara appears in numerous Upanishads and in Buddhism, Hinduism and Jainism and in early Vedic texts like the Rigveda and in the Bhagavad Gita, as in XVIII, 61:

iishvaraH	*sarva*	*bhuutaanaaM*	*hrd*	*deshe*	*Arjuna*	*tishthati*
Self	of all	beings	heart	region		resides

bhraamayan	*sarva*	*bhuutaani*	*yantra*	*aaruudhaani*	*maayayaa*
revolving	all	beings	machine	as mounted on	by delusion

The Self resides in the hearts of all beings, causing them all to revolve, by its illusive power, as if they were mounted on a machine. (2)

"Maayayaa" can be also be translated as "through Maya" or "as if by magic".

"Mandala" literally translates as "circle", but represents the universe, the cosmos and the interactions of all the forces that create it.

There is a Tibetan Vajrayana sand-painting practice where monks take many days constructing an elaborate mandala, painstakingly detailing the wonders and complexities of the universe. When it is completed, it is swept up and thrown it into a body of water, symbolizing the impermanence of life and its transcendence. As the 14th century Dzogchen master, Longchengpa Rabjempa said, "Where there is no you, there is no mandala", a perfect demonstration of nonduality. (3)

WHERE DOES THE CONCEPT OF A "BODY" COME FROM?

mana	eva	mahad	duhkhaM	mana	eva	shariirakam
mind	alone	great	sorrow	mind	alone	cause of body

mana	eva	prapancaakhyaM	mana eva	kalebaram
mind	alone	is the world	mind alone	is the body

Mind, indeed, is the great sorrow. Mind, indeed, is the cause of the body.
Mind, indeed, is the world of phenomena. Mind, indeed, is the body.
Mind and its capabilities to remember the past and project the future with its
stories, fears, and attachments cause the great sorrow in our lives.

"Prapancaakhyam" translates as the five-fold world, the classical model of "earth, water, fire, air and ether", used in ancient Greece, Egypt, Babylonia, Tibet, Japan and India. It is used throughout the Ribhu Gita. The mind creates the "world" from these five elements.

The mind similarly creates this concept of a "body" as a discrete, single assemblage of many, many components. (1)

Ramana Maharshi emphasized the nature of the mind as nothing more than a collection of thoughts, based on the "I". His magnum opus, *Upadesa Saram*, describes the process of analyzing the mind and the surprising result:

Verse 17:

maanasaM	tu	kiM	maargane	krte
mind	exactly	what is	inquiry	is undertaken

na-	iva	maanasaM	maargaH	aarjavaat
not	at all	mind	path	direct

When an inquiry is made into what this mind is, it will be found that there is no mind at all. This is the direct path for realization of the Self.

Verse 18:

vrttayaH-	*tv-*	*ahaM*	*vrttim-*	*aashritaaH*
thoughts	but	I	thought	are dependent upon

vrttayaH	*manaH*	*viddhi-*	*ahaM*	*manaH*
thoughts	mind	know that	I	mind

Your thoughts are dependent upon the "I- thought".
The mind is nothing but thoughts. Know that the "I" is the mind.

WHERE DOES THE FEELING OF A "KNOT" IN OUR HEART COME FROM?

dehe	*aham*	*iti*	*sankalpaH*	*hrdydaya*	*granthir*	*iritaH*
body	I am	this	notion	heart	knot	is regarded

kaala	*trayepi*	*tanna asti*	*sarvam*	*brahma*	*eti*	*kevalam*
time	three periods	is not	all	Brahman	is	alone

The notion "I am the body" is regarded as the "heart knot".
In all the three periods of time, it is not so. All is Self, alone.

"sankalpaH" has many translations, from "determination" to "notion" to "deeply held fact". The "notion" translation will be used as it is not a "deeply held fact" or a "determination", just a mistaken perception.

The "heart knot" is an important principle in spiritual literature. As Ramana Maharshi says "there is a connection between the source of the various psychic nerves and the Self, that this is the knot of the heart, that the connection between the sentient and the insentient will exist until this is cut asunder with the aid of true knowledge, that just as the subtle and invisible force of electricity travels through wires and does many wonderful things, so the force of the Self also travels through the psychic nerves and, pervading the entire body, imparts sentience to the senses, and that if this knot is untied the Self will remain as it always is, without any attributes." (1)

"Three periods of time" are past, present and future, i.e. it was not true in the past, is not true now, and will never be true.

Where does the sense of different bodies come from?

dehe	*tri*	*epi*	*bhaavam*	*yat*	*tad*	*deha*	*jnanam*	*ucyate*
body	three-fold		supposition	that	that	body	knowledge	is said

kaala	*trayepi*	*tanna asti*	*sarvam*	*brahma*	*eti*	*kevalam*
time	three periods	is not	all	Brahman	is	alone

The supposition that "I am the three-fold body" is said to be the knowledge of the body.
In all the three periods of time, it is not so. All is Self, alone.

Bhaavam is often translated as "notion", or "idea", but "supposition" carries a better sense of the meaning here.

The "three fold body" is what is called the "anthroposophical view", as "temporal body, evolving soul and eternal spirit".

Eternal spirit evolves by becoming progressively more awakened to Self-consciousness through its reflection on the deeds and suffering of a physical body.

As far as "evolving soul", with the disappearance of the "I", it is apparent that many serendipities and precognitions of infinitesimal probability and great value manifest every day. Clearly, "something" is running things that is far more intelligent, omnipresent, and interconnected than am i. "my life" runs better without "me" in it.

Current cosmological research demonstrates that an all-pervasive field, called the Higgs field, for which a Nobel Prize was awarded, exists that can manifest matter. (1) As everything in this Field (which is everything) is evolving, then whatever is running things is also evolving. The sensing-experiencing manifestations of this Field allow It/Her to evolve.

The Field is also likely to be "self-conscious", as several species are, as parts of the Field could not have properties that the Field did not have, likely with enhanced capabilities. This would make serendipities and precognitions much easier to explain.

Temporal body is the aspects of human existence that endure for a single lifetime, also called the etheric body. (2)

The title of the book, *Evolving Beyond Thought*, reflects the role that evolution has played in creating our current highly-problematic software, with its self-referential internal narrative, and what might be done to continue to evolve and move beyond those limitations.

Where does the sense of "real" and "unreal" originate?

dehe   aham   iti   yad   bhaavam   sad   asad   bhaavam   eva   ca
body   I am   this that supposition real not real supposition verily and

kaala   trayepi   anna asti sarvam   brahma   eti   kevalam
time   three periods is not   all   Brahman   is   alone

The supposition "I am this body" creates the supposition of "real" and "not real".
In all the three periods of time, it is not so.   All is Self, alone.

If we didn't have the concept of a body, and the belief that it was us, how could we conceive of something being "real" and something not being "real". The blogpost "What is really 'real'? What does 'nothing is real' mean?" describes my personal experience:

> "When i say that 'nothing is real', that is my ongoing direct perception. i can recognize trees as different from sky, and chairs from lamps, and avoid bumping into the furniture (normally) but there is a deep experiential, not philosophical, 'knowing', and direct seeing that they are not 'material', not really 'real'. They appear to all have the same 'energy', and to be, at some level, all one thing, like they were in a painting. There is at the same time, a deep Stillness that is unchanging, 'underneath' all this.

This insight has been reported by mystics for millennia, and doubtless those who have used psychedelics (i haven't) can resonate with this." (1)

These different appearances of "reality" are heavily influenced by the activity of the key networks in the brain and which ones are activated or deactivated.

my ongoing perception is basically "psychedelic" if the head is not moving much. Moving the head appears to engage the Tasking Network. When the head is still, it appears to be in the Default Mode Network (DMN), which, in my case, has a deactivated "self and other" sub-network, so "All is One".

Another sub-network of the DMN, which creates the sense of an entity that goes through time, is also deactivated so there is only living "now, now, now". Also, a different "reality". (2) (3)

Our brain wasn't evolved to generate an accurate depiction of what's there, only one that is evolutionarily useful. As Tor Norretranders points out in "Inside Out: The Epistemology of Everything":

> "What we perceive as being outside of us is a fancy and elegant projection of what we have inside; everything we experience is inside...The trick of perception is the trick of mistaking an inner world for the outside world...When we understand that the inner emotional states are more real than what we experience of the outside world, the epoch of insane mania for rational control will be over." (4)

Some contemporary physicists are coming to the conclusion described earlier that what is "real", and underlying all of this, is an all-pervasive, "self-aware", Field of Universal Consciousness.

If IT is everything, IT is communicating with Itself, and is "everywhere" and "everything". It seems impossible to ever know "ITs" state as it is more intelligent than we will be able to grasp. Also, since we are IT, we cannot stand "outside" of IT and "understand" IT. (5)

WHERE DOES THE IDEA THAT THERE IS A WORLD COME FROM?

dehe	*aham*	*iti*	*sankalpaH*	*tat*	*prapancaami*		*hocyate*
body	I am	this	notion	that	world of five elements		is said

kaala	*trayepi*	*tanna asti*	*sarvam*	*brahma*	*eti*	*kevalam*
time	three periods	is not	all	Brahman	is	alone

The notion that "I am this body" creates the manifest world (of the five elements). In all the three periods of time, it is not so. All is Self, alone.

When we believe we are the body, it brings with it a manifest world within which this body functions and interacts. Without this concept of being a body, the manifest world is clearly seen and perceived to be an illusion.

This world of the five elements as described earlier is the classical model of "earth, water, fire, air and ether", which has been used in ancient Greece, Egypt, Babylonia, Tibet, Japan and India. (1)

As discussed in the previous verse, we do know from our research studies on the default mode network (DMN) that there is a network that evolved to create the illusion of separation between us and other objects and us as an entity passing through time. When the DMN is deactivated by self-inquiry, the serotonergic psychedelics, or other "mystical" means, the perceived world is seen without the brain's evolved distorting circuitry as a mere illusory construct. When the DMN withers, the fictional strategies of this illusory world are no longer convincing.

WHAT IS THE FUNDAMENTAL SOURCE OF OUR MISUNDERSTANDINGS?

dehe	*aham*	*iti*	*sankalpaH*	*tat*	*eva*	*ajnanam*	*ucyate*
body	I am	this	notion	that	alone	ignorance	is said to

kaala	*trayepi*		*tanna asti*	*sarvam*	*brahma*	*eti*	*kevalam*
time	three periods		is not	all	Brahman	is	alone

The notion that "I am this body", alone, is said to be ignorance.
In all the three periods of time, it is not so. All is Self, alone.

This belief that we are these bodies is the fundamental ignorance about ourselves and this world around us and in which we appear to function. It is the root cause of our lack of understanding of our True Nature and the Self.

WHERE DO OUR BIASES AND MISCONCEPTIONS COME FROM?

dehe	*aham*	*iti*	*yaa*	*buddhiH*		*malinaa*	*vaasan*	*ucyate*
body	I am	this	that	intellectual conclusion		impurities	impressions	is said

kaala	*trayepi*		*tanna asti*	*sarvam*	*brahma*	*eti*	*kevalam*
time	three periods		is not	all	Brahman	is	alone

The intellectual conclusion that "I am this body" is said to be the cause of impurities and impressions.
In all the three periods of time, it is not so. All is Self, alone.

The misconception that we are these bodies brings with it distorted memories, fears and stories of the past which makes clear perception of our life and truly "skillful" action impossible. The neuroscience research on our inability to recall the "past" correctly, overwhelmingly demonstrates just how poor our memories are. The blogpost "How neuroscience, psychological studies and our poor memories change the law…" gives some indication of just how poor our memories are and how much they are distorted as they are recalled several times.

As subjects in an fMRI study of "faulty memory", we were given four seconds to "grade" by like/not like, etc. a memory of a backpack, lamp, etc. for an hour. The next day they were shown at a similar pace and we rated how well, and by what feature, we remembered them, or not. Although some were remembered well, one part of those just didn't "feel" like it belonged there. It didn't. That is called "false memory".

Each time a memory is recalled, the brain assembles an evolutionarily most-useful picture, with all of the information it has stored that may be somehow related to the current situation from all the times that situation or a similar one occurred.

It was evolutionarily critical to generate "most useful" memories, not "most correct" memories. Our brains evolved to put in elements from other similar memories that may enhance survivability. Fifty thousand years ago in eastern Africa, how perfect the trees around the watering hole were was less "useful" for our survival than noticing brown patches in the grasses or strange bumps in the water.

Astute attorneys and law enforcement personnel have used this understanding to "plant" false memories in eye witnesses' memories. With some reinforcement, that false memory will become the new "reality".

Without the belief that "I am this body", these distorted episodic memories could likely not have been created. (1)

WHERE DOES THE IDEA THAT WE ARE A SEPARATE INDIVIDUAL COME FROM?

dehe	aham	iti	yaa	buddhiH		satyaM	jivaH		sa
eva	saH								
body	I am	this	that	intellectual	conclusion	truly	individual soul	that	
alone	is								

kaala	trayepi		tanna asti	sarvam	brahma	eti	kevalam
time	three periods		is not	all	Brahman	is	alone

The intellectual conclusion that "I am this body" truly, alone, is the individual soul.
In all the t   hree periods of time, it is not so. All is Self, alone.

The evolution of the "subject/doing/object" concept and its symbolic logic about 75,000 years ago made possible communication and the unique ability to assign complex tasks to large groups, and then to subsequently change them. This "first of its kind" capability with its "I" software , the very heart of the creation of the "individual soul", made our species tremendously evolutionarily successful.

Without the creation of a "someone" who has a body, an "individual soul" with all of its problems, concerns, worries, etc. would never have manifested. It may be the software that, with its supportive malware programs, particularly confirmation bias, as described in the first section of the book, destines our species for an early exit. The average mammalian species lasts about 1 million years; Homo sapiens has existed for 200,000 to 300,000 years. What's the bet on another 700,000 years? (1) (2)

HOW DOES THIS BELIEF THAT WE ARE THESE BODIES, MANIFEST IN OUR LIVES?

dehe	aham	iti	sankalpaH	maha	anarakam		iiritam
body	I am	this	notion	great	hell		is proclaimed

kaala	trayepi	tanna asti	sarvam	brahma	eti	kevalam
time	three periods	is not	all	Brahman	is	alone

The notion that "I am this body" is proclaimed as the "great hell".
In all the three periods of time, it is not so.   All is Self, alone.

A powerful verse summing up most folks' experience with their belief that they are their bodies.

Contemporary culture, and to some extent evolution, focuses on making "our" bodies beautiful and matching some idealized model reinforced by mass marketing. This is a "great hell" if folk are strongly attached to that appearance.

Working with a young woman who was strongly attached to her attractiveness, i asked what she would do if she lost an arm. She quickly replied "I would kill myself". When asked about a finger, the same answer emerged.

The inevitable, natural decline in the body as it ages can be that "great hell" if we are strongly identified with our attractiveness.   Struggling against this decline, folk use plastic surgery, injections, liposuction, lotions, diets, exercise programs, etc., desperate in an ultimately-futile exercise.

Some fingers typing this line are mangled, others are genetically-distorted. This body has many maladies. These have been great gifts, particularly the mangled finger, which made it impossible to continue with golf, which had been a serious attachment. It freed up many hours for meditation and yoga and made it clear that "i am not this body" as nothing changed in Consciousness.

Deconstructing the "I am this body" belief, we escape this "great hell" of fears, anxieties, stories, depression, etc. and live a life of Bliss, Stillness and "now, now, now".

WHERE DOES OUR CONCEPT OF A "MIND" COME FROM?

dehe	aham	iti	yaa	buddhiH	mana	eviti	nishcitam
body	I am	this	that	assertion	mind	is only	defined

kaala	trayepi	tanna asti	sarvam	brahma	eti	kevalam
time	three periods	is not	all	Brahman	is	alone

*The assertion "I am this body" is defined as certainly being the mind.
In all the three periods of time, it is not so. All is Self, alone.*

This mind is defined and created by the belief that "I am this body". Without this belief, there would be no need for a concept of a "mind" to manage, direct and maintain the body. The body evolved to protect itself and did so successfully for millennia before the "I" concept manifested. As pointed out earlier, the on-line, conscious "rider" of the ego/I has only 1/500,000 of the processing capability of the off-line "elephant" which does 99.99% of the operation of the body "all by itself".

As Ramana Maharshi states in *Upadesa Saram*, if we inquire into what the mind actually is, we will find that is only a collection of thoughts:

Verse 17:

maanasaM	tu	kiM	maargane	krte
mind	exactly	what is	inquiry	is undertaken

na-	iva	maanasaM	maargaH	aarjavaat
not	at all	mind	path	straight, direct

If an inquiry is made into what the mind is, it will be found that there is no mind. This is the direct path for Self-realization.

Verse 18:

vrttayas-	*tv-*	*ahaM*	*vrttim-*	*aashritaaH*	
thoughts	but	"I"	thought	are dependent upon	

vrttayaH	*mano*	*viddhya-*	*ahaM*	*manaH*
thoughts	mind	know that	"I"	mind

Thoughts alone make up the mind and depend on the "I" thought. Know that the "I" thought constitutes the mind. (1)

Looking at those thoughts, the problematic, self-referential narrative ones all contain an I/me/my creating desires and fears by imagining the future or re-constructing the past. It may have been useful when the dangers were "lions and tigers and bears" or the folk in the next cave.

However, in today's staggeringly complex, massively-interconnected world, the dangers are mentally created from countless information sources of questionable credibility, instantaneously, on everything, everywhere. Even minor happenings on the other side of the world, about which we can do nothing, are constantly updated and sensationally discussed in great detail, until the next one arises in a few minutes. This generates continual anxiety, stress and unhappiness in a futile exercise.

WHY DO WE BELIEVE WE ARE DIFFERENT FROM EVERYTHING ELSE?

dehe	*aham*	*iti*	*yaa*	*buddhiH*	*paricchinnam*	*itiiryate*
body	I am	this	that	assertion	the limitation	regarded as

kaala	*trayepi*	*tanna asti*	*sarvam*	*brahma*	*eti*	*kevalam*
time	three periods	is not	all	Brahman	is	alone

The assertion that "I am this body" is the limitation. In all the three periods of time, it is not so. All is Self, alone.

This "I am this body" concept defines our identity and limitations, and separates us by age, size, gender, skin color, attractiveness, health, infirmities, etc. from others. If we did not "buy into" those attributes as meaningful, what would our identity, or limitations be?

A powerful exercise is to imagine ourselves as 20 years older or younger, 30 pounds heavier or lighter, with several different skin colors, six inches taller or shorter, a different gender with different sexual preferences, living in different countries, and different centuries. Watch how the "identify" shifts in each case. What are we really without those "limitations"?

This "I am this body" concept also creates and defines a demarcation between this body and other bodies, trees, cars, animals, buildings, etc. Can we imagine ourselves as that tree, dog, cat, lion, etc.? Just how are we different from it?

As discussed earlier, a sub-network in the Default Mode Network creates the sense of "self and other". If this sub-network is deactivated by meditation, mystical experiences, or psychedelics, or if the "I" concept is deconstructed, there is no neural functioning to generate this limitation. (1)

Without this "I am this body" limitation, the mystical experience of "All is One" manifests, temporarily or permanently. Explore this possibility carefully and see what it means for your individual identity.

WHERE DO OUR SORROWS COME FROM?

dehe	aham	iti	yad	jnaanaM	sarvaM	shoka	itiiritam
body	I am	this	that	knowledge	all	sorrow	described

kaala	trayepi	tanna asti	sarvam	brahma	eti	kevalam
time	three periods	is not	all	Brahman	is	alone

The (mis)understanding that "I am this body" is described as all-sorrowful.
In all the three periods of time, it is not so. All is Self, alone.

Do all of our sorrows come from this mistaken understanding that "I am this body"?

Can you remember a sorrow that wasn't tied to this belief in the body being what you are? What would trauma, illnesses, disease, failed relationships, unemployment, or loss of loved ones be like if you were not attached to this belief that you were this body? Remember, or imagine, how quickly your "identity" changes when you receive a "good" or "bad" prognosis for a serious illness or disease, and then when it was subsequently reversed.

Isn't it clear that suicide is a decision that the "I"makes that some great suffering only exists because of the body's existence and that if it were done away with, all would be fine? Just look carefully and see how that belief arises from the ego/I's distortions, stories, fears, etc. generating those sorrows? If the ego/I realized it would not be present for the funeral, and was only an outdated program running on a second-rate processor with little functional value or meaningful contribution, would this decision even arise? (1) (2) (3)

WHAT IS THE GREAT MISTAKE THAT THE "I" MAKES?

dehe	aham	iti	yad	jnaanaM	saMsparshamiti	kathyate
body	I am	this	that	understanding	great (mis)touch	talked about

kaala	trayepi	tanna asti	sarvam	brahma	eti	kevalam
time	three periods	is not	all	Brahman	is	alone

The (mis)understanding that "I am this body" is said to be the great conflict.
In all the three periods of time, it is not so. All is Self, alone.

This great mis-touch, or mis-take, of assuming that the body needs the "I" to function successfully, is a great distortion and error as discussed earlier. The body functions "just fine" without the "conscious" involvement of the "I" with its seriously limited processing power and data handling capability and endless talking to, judging, and arguing with itself, about itself.

As discussed earlier, the blogpost "Right-sizing your "I", understanding confirmation bias...new studies" discussed the great mismatch between the "online", ego/I's processor and the "off line" parallel processing power of the brain, and how virtually everything is done without the conscious "I"'s involvement, awareness or understanding. (1) (2)

Watch as "your" hand moves - do you have any idea how that is happening? How do the ligaments, tendons, muscles, blood, skin, sensory signals, neural chemistry, etc. coordinate and manifest this mysterious, magical, and yet so common activity?

Watch as "you" walk. How does that happen so seamlessly, navigating around obstacles, compensating for going up and down steps, dealing with different surfaces, etc.? Do you have any clue how that very complex activity occurs?

Do you consciously manage the processes to eat, digest your food, breathe, manufacture waste, see, hear or speak?

How can anyone seriously believe that "they" are consciously required for the body's activities except on an "after the fact" basis as they are virtually always somewhere else in their mind? This is clearly a great mis-touch, and mis-take.

Where does the idea of "death" come from?

dehe	aham	iti	yaa	buddhiH	tadeva	maranaM	smrtam
body	I am	this	that	assertion	that verily	death	understood

kaala	trayepi	tanna asti	sarvam	brahma	eti	kevalam
time	three periods	is not	all	Brahman	is	alone

The assertion that "I am this body" is itself understood to create death.
In all the three periods of time, it is not so. All is Self, alone.

If we did not believe we were these bodies, would we have any concept of "dying" or "death" when the body decayed or stopped functioning?

Do those species that don't have self-referential consciousness have the ongoing angst of "death" that our species does? Do you see birds worrying and distressed about how old they are and how long they have left to live? Are they concerned about their "life's purpose" and whether they fulfilled it? Or do they just go about being, in the moment, without dread, worry, or fear of "dying", functioning at the limit of their capabilities until those bodies cease working?

As one proceeds on this path of nondual awakening by deconstructing the ego/I concept, the common report is that there is an increasingly clear understanding that "I do not die." What better demonstration could there be of the truth of this verse in the Ribhu Gita?

The Bhagavad Gita in Chapter II, Verse 27 discusses this anxiety about death:

jaatasya	hi	dhruvo	mrtyuH	dhruvam	janma	mrtasya	ca
those born	for	certain	death	certain	birth	those dead	and

tasmaat	aparihaarye	arthe	na	tvam	shocitum	arhasi
therefore	over an inevitable	fact	not	you	to grieve	ought

Whoever is born, for him, death is certain, and whoever dies, for him, birth is certain. Therefore there is no point in grieving over what is inevitable. (1)

The classical reincarnation belief is that "you" as an individual entity will be reborn, carrying over the fruits of your actions from life to life. There are, however, many scientific, logical and "bookkeeping" issues regarding what it is that is carried over, and how and by whom would one's "good deeds" and "bad deeds" be weighed and evaluated.

We cannot know all sources of all elements of any action of ours or others. It is impossible to know all effects on countless unknown others, and their actions on others, as an action dances forward through space-time. What may be a small "bad" happening to "me", may result in future "good", "bad" or "indifferent" happenings to others. How could the results of all of those happenings be known, let alone meaningfully evaluated?

An alternative interpretation, which i find much more likely, and surprisingly comforting, is that when the physical body goes away, whatever remains is absorbed into the ocean of Self, the Field of Universal Consciousness.

There is now no one "here" that wants, needs, or merits continuing. Whatever learning has occurred in, of and by the Self, has already been integrated into the vast Field of Universal Consciousness where it affects the memes of "everything" now and in the future. No continuation of an individual entity is meaningful.

WHAT IS WRONG WITH THE IDEA THAT "I AM THIS BODY"?

dehe	aham	iti	yaa	buddhiH	tadeva	ashobhanaM	smrtam
body	I am	this	that	assertion	that verily	inauspicious	understood

kaala	trayepi	tanna asti	sarvam	brahma	eti	kevalam
time	three periods	is not	all	Brahman	is	alone

The assertion "I am this body" is regarded as inauspicious.
In all the three periods of time, it is not so. All is Self, alone.

The term "ashobhanaM" is also translated as "unpleasant".

After the preceding verse, this seems anticlimactic, almost. However, "inauspicious" is more serious than it might appear. It is also translated as "ill omened", "ominous", and "future success is unlikely". The last verse's "creation of the concept of death" from the belief that "I am this body", is now extended to one's future while alive, which, if that belief that "(s)he is this body" continues, will make "future success unlikely".

As discussed earlier, if we are obsessed with the appearance, condition and desirability of our physical form, we are assured of "unlikely" future success. Our bodies will deteriorate and fail, no matter what we do to try to slow or prevent its changes. This is certain to be "unpleasant", and the stronger our "inauspicious" belief is that we are these bodies, the more we will suffer.

JUST HOW SERIOUS IS THIS MISTAKEN BELIEF THAT "I AM THIS BODY"?

dehe	*aham*	*iti*	*yaa*	*buddhiH*	*maha*	*apaapamiti*	*smrtam*
body	I am	this	that	assertion	great	sin	understood

kaala	*trayepi*	*tanna asti*	*sarvam*	*brahma*	*eti*	*kevalam*
time	three periods	is not	all	Brahman	is	alone

The assertion that "I am this body" is understood to be a/the great sin.
In all the three periods of time, it is not so. All is Self, alone.

The Judeo-Christian conditioning on "sin", seminal to "my" childhood, originated from "sin" or "syn" from the Biblical Greek or Roman word "*hamartia*" for "failure, missing the mark, being in error". The Hebrew "*hata*" for "sin" originated from archery and literally referred to missing the "gold" at the center of the target. (1) (2)

This provides a more useful vision of not reaching the "gold" of nondual awakening. Throughout the Ribhu Gita, the focus is on removing deeply-conditioned and heavily-supported beliefs from religions, institutions, cultures, merchandising, etc. of being identified with, and as, body, thoughts or mind.

Believing that one's body is what one is, one faces the "great sin" of being misled to pursue society's targets of desirable genetic partners, power and wealth. Instead, focus on the target of going beyond suffering, realize that you are not this body, and hit the "gold" at the center of the target of the Bliss and Stillness of nondual awakening.

WHY IS THIS CONCEPT SO OVERWHELMING?

dehe	*aham*	*iti*	*yaa*	*buddhiH*	*tushthaa*		*saiva*	*hi*	*cocyate*
body	I am	this	that	assertion	great prejudiced conception		verily	is	said

kaala	*trayepi*	*tanna asti*	*sarvam*	*brahma*	*eti*	*kevalam*
time	three periods	is not	all	Brahman	is	alone

The assertion is "I am this body" is, verily, overwhelming, it is said.
In all the three periods of time, it is not so. All is Self, alone.

The translation of "*tushthaa saiva*" is difficult with "overwhelming" and "a great prejudiced conception" being the best options. "Overwhelming" is used as this belief that "I am this body" does overwhelm our mind, thinking, perspectives, etc.

One of the great surprises when the problematic, self-referential internal-narrative thoughts stopped like a light switch was thrown, was that it was clear that virtually all of those thoughts arose from this belief that "I am this body". The stopping occurred when a yoga posture flow/vinyasa series was being done with the focus on the negation "I am not this body" while inverted in a complex shoulderstand. Click, it was true, the switch was thrown, the "last penny dropped", and it has been that way for 19 years.

During a presentation at a Science and Nonduality Conference, this was described but there was no information given on the posture which was being done. Afterwards, in the hallway, one of the most celebrated scientists working on the neurophysiology of the human brain and the practice of meditation, who was at the presentation, came up to me and guessed it.

Focusing our self-inquiry and "letting-go" practices on this erroneous belief and the attachments it creates, our self-referential thoughts quickly become fewer, less sticky, and less problematic, even if complete stopping is not reached. It is only "overwhelming" if we do not seriously investigate this belief and dis-empower the ego/I's creations.

DOES THE "I AM THIS BODY" BELIEF CAUSE ALL OF MY "FAULTS"?

dehe	aham	iti	sankalpaH	sarva	dosham	iti	smrtam
body	I am	this	notion	all	faults	is	understood

kaala	trayepi	tanna asti	sarvam	brahma	eti	kevalam
time	three periods	is not	all	Brahman	is	alone

The notion that "I am this body" is understood to be all defects.
In all the three periods of time, it is not so. All is Self, alone.

The term "dosha" has different meanings depending upon context. Currently, in yogic and "new age" circles, it is known in the Ayurvedic medicine perspective of three energies circulating in the body which govern physiological activity. Much time, energy and money has been expended on determining and controlling your pitta, vata and kapha. It covers at least the first 10 Google search pages. (1)

However, in the Advaitic perspective, it means "fault, vice, deficiency, want, wickedness, sinfulness". (2) This reflects the previous verses as the "I am this body" concept is identified as the cause of the overwhelming faults which cause one to miss the "gold" of attaining the state of nondual awakening and its Sat, Chit and Ananda, or Being, Consciousness and Bliss.

Ramana Maharshi said, re "dosha":

"If one asks 'Who am I? How did I get this dosha (fault) of life?', then there will be Self-realization. Dosha will get eliminated and shanti will be obtained. Why even obtained? It (the Self) remains as It IS". (3)

Ramana Maharshi gives in his "Upadesa Saram", this direct path to under-standing this "dosha":

Verse 19.

aham	ayaM	kutaH	bhavati	cinvataH
"I"	this	from where	is born	inquiring into

ayi	patati	aham	nija	vicaaranam
Oh!	falls	"I"	self	inquiry

Inquiring into where this "I" comes from,
Oh! The "I" falls away. This is self-inquiry.

And in verse 20, he describes the surprising result:

ahami	naashabhaaji-	aham ahantayaa
"I"	is destroyed	"I – I"

sphurati	hrt-	svayaM	parama-	puurna-	sat
shines	from the Heart	by itself	supreme	complete	Being

When the "I" is deconstructed, there shines forth, by itself, the Self as "I-I", as the supreme, complete Being.

IF I'M NOT THIS BODY, THEN WHAT AM I?

The previous verses were negations of what we are not - not these thoughts with their problems, not this mind with its distortions, not this identification with the body which cause so many difficulties. The next eight verses are about what the "Ground of all Being", Self, Aatman, Brahman, Universal Consciousness/She is, and what its characteristics are.

If the "I/self" is deconstructed, this Self/Universal Consciousness/She is revealed to have been there all along and what "we" are.

Many folk feel uncomfortable, or egotistical, with this concept, depending on how much work remains to be done to deconstruct their ego/I. With continued perseverance in self-inquiry and letting-go of attachments, it will become true, natural, and continuous, without any "ownership" or "doing". It is important to remember that not only are "you" the Self, but so is everything and everyone else and it has always been that way.

The Bhagavad Gita gives a very popular and concise definition of what the Self is in Chapter 10, Verse 20:

| aham- | aatmaa | gudaakesha | sarva- | bhuuta- | ashaya- | sthitaH |
| I am | the Self | always present | all | beings | heart | resides |

| aham | adish | ca | madhyaM | ca | bhuutaanaam | anta | eva | ca |
| I am | creator | and | sustainer | and | all beings | dissolver | even | and |

I am the Self dwelling in the Hearts of all beings.
I am the creator, sustainer and dissolver of all beings.

The second line can also be interpreted as "I am the beginning, the middle and the end of all beings". (1)

The Self is in the hearts of everyone. It is the birth, the life, and the death of all. This is one of the most cited and powerful verses in the Bhagavad Gita. Two Indian sages of the 20th century, Ramana Maharshi and Ramesh Balsekar, said that this verse alone could be chosen as the sole focus of meditation to reach awakening.

Another key verse from the Bhagavad Gita for looking for the Self in everyday life is in Chapter 13, Verse 27:

samam	sarveshu	bhuuteshu	tishthantam	parameshvaram
equally	in all	beings	residing	the Self

vinashyatsu	avinashyantam	yaH	pashyati	saH	pashyati
among the perishable	the imperishable	one	who sees	(s)he	sees

(s)he who sees the Self, residing equally in all beings – the imperishable among the perishable – the unchanging among the changing, sees clearly. (2)

Any day, watch for what does not change. Whether it is mountains, oceans, rocks, trees, folk, plants, animals, earth, emotions, desires, fears, sensations, etc., just keep asking "Does this change?" Something, something, doesn't change…find it.

It is easiest to see Her, in my experience, by looking between objects rather than at them. Use the objects, including the breath and thoughts, as pointers to where She is "unmanifested" as the Bhagavad Gita says. She is everywhere, but is most obvious in the gaps and spaces.

There are many descriptions of the attributes of the Self in the Bhagavad Gita (including this one that was useful when rafting the Grand Canyon) in Chapter 2, Verse 24:

acchedyaH	ayam	adaahyaH	ayam	akledyaH	ashoshyaH
cannot be cut	Self	cannot burn	Self	cannot be wetted	cannot be dried

eva   ca
also   and

nityaH sarva gataH   sthaanuH   acalaH   ayaM   sanaatanaH
eternal all   pervading immovable unmoving   Self   changeless

The Self cannot be cut, burnt, wetted or dried. It is eternal, all pervading, immovable, unmoving, and changeless. (3)

The refrain for the Ribhu Gita verses in this section begins with "aanadaM paramaM manam" translated as "Bliss is the primary measure" of whether one has reached the persistent nondual state. As that was "my" direct experience, the first book was titled "Happiness Beyond Thought".

The refrain to every verse in Nirvana Shatakam, a key Advaitic text included in that book, is "cit ananda rupahaH" or "I am Bliss Consciousness". It appears in many texts as "sat chit ananda" or "satchitananda" translated as "existence, consciousness, and bliss", the traditional description of the ultimate, unchanging reality of the Self.

This is an important distinction between nondual awakening and many other religious and spiritual traditions and practices, which have goals like "compassion", "love" or "not sinning". Nondual awakening is all about the "Bliss".

What is my nature?

aham	*eva*	*hi*	*gupta*	*atmaa*	*aham*	*eva*	*nirantaram*
I am	alone	truly	mysterious	Self	I am	alone	gapless

aanandaM	*paramaM*	*maanam*	*idaM*	*dRshyaM*	*na*	*kincana*
bliss	supreme	measure	all this	that is seen	not	anything

I am alone the mysterious Self. I am alone the gapless.
Bliss is the supreme measure. All this which is seen is not anything.

"Gupta" can also be translated as "secret", which does not capture the real essence of the Self, and creates separation from the goal. If something is "secret", then it becomes a carefully-guarded, obscure practice doled out by "superior" folk with titles, special hats, hairdos and garb, for a price, increasing with the level of "attainment".

That is not the reality. Although it is impossible to accurately describe, like the smell of a rose, the Self can be found, on a DIY basis, through free, non-secret, practices like self-inquiry and "letting go" of attachments.

"Nirantaram" can also be translated as "interstice-less", which is cumbersome and obscure. "Gapless" more accurately describes the reality that there is no space where the Self is not. There is not a Self here and a Self over there… it is all Self, even, and particularly easy to see, in the spaces between objects, thoughts and breaths.

As far as "na kincana", "not anything" is used rather than "nothing" as it better conveys the absence of something transient, rather than that there was never anything there. This is a frequent misinterpretation and creates much misunderstanding as in Buddhism in the Heart Sutra where "shuunyata" is translated as "Void" as discussed earlier. What **is there** is the ultimate, unchanging Reality and nothing could be added, or taken away from it, to improve it.

What is the ultimate teacher?

aham	eva	paraM	brahma	aham	eva	guror guruH
I am	alone	supreme	Brahman	I am	alone	the Guru of gurus

aanandaM	paramaM	maanam	idaM	dRshyaM	na	kincana
bliss	supreme	measure	all this	that is seen	is	nothing

I am, alone, the supreme Brahman. I am, alone, the Guru of gurus.
Bliss is the supreme measure. All this which is seen is not anything.

Obviously, "guru of gurus", can be "teacher of teachers". The real questions are how "teaching" manifests, what it accomplishes, and who it is really for, the teacher or the student?

The most useful teachers teach others how to learn. my principal Ph.D. thesis advisor taught by "abandonment". Some funding was provided along with a broad problem outline, and then you solve it. Designing and constructing equipment, assembling disparate resources from various faculty and facilities, developing new approaches, processes, and measurements, etc. was all DIY. That process produced the best long-term outcomes in our department which was #1 or #2 in the world.

IME, DIY works best for nondual awakening as each folk's path is unique given their different backgrounds, genetics, conditioning, skills, abilities, previous practices, etc. It is also how thousands of hours of yoga, meditation, etc. unfolded in my process with little direct guidance as there was no other alternative.

Ramana Maharshi transmitted his teaching mostly through "presence" and silence. As Ramana Maharshi said:

"Q. There are great men, public workers who cannot solve the problem of the misery of the world.

M. They are ego-centered; hence their inability. If they remained in the Self, they would be different.

Q. Why do enlightened persons not help?

M. How do you know that they do not help? Public speeches, physical activity, and material help are all outweighed by the silence of the enlightened persons. They accomplish more than others." (1)

As far as selecting "spiritual" teachers, make certain that they have "walked the walk, not just talked the talk". Did they do those practices and get in those states, or are they just parroting what they've heard or (mis)remember of an experience?

Every time a memory of an experience is recalled, it changes as it is modified by our brains to incorporate "useful" information from other experiences that would enhance our survivability in similar situations. As discussed earlier, this leads to the ability of skillful attorneys and law enforcement folk to plant "false memories" in our memories of experiences. This has led to questioning guidelines in some states to limit this manipulation.

There are many teachers and exhaustive content available in many formats so great confusion is inevitable. There is also much misrepresentation, manipulation and exploitation. Without any guidelines, oversight, credentialing, etc., it really is "buyer beware".

A good approach is to spend time around someone, and see if, at your deepest level, you really "trust" them. Our brains evolved great capacity to rapidly analyze body language and speech for just this process as our survival depended on it. Listen carefully to the "intuition" from the off-line "elephant" and not the on-line ego/I "rider", yours or your friends as discussed earlier.

Toni Packer, my one Rinzai Zen teacher, was described as "...a Zen teacher minus the 'teacher' and minus the 'Zen'". That is why her work was so useful. (2)

It is also important to remember that the best teachers may be your family, friends, partners, roomies, the clerk at Trader Joes, the folk in line at the DMV, fremenies, etc. Remember, Universal Consciousness/She is everywhere in everyone...everyone.

What is the ultimate happiness?

aham	eva	akhilaa	adhaara	aham	eva	sukhaat sukham
I am	alone	whole	support	I am	alone	happiness beyond happiness

aanandaM	paramaM	maanam	idaM	dRshyaM	na	kincana
bliss	supreme	measure	all this	that is seen	is	nothing

I am, alone, the support of everything. I am, alone, the happiness beyond happiness. Bliss is the supreme measure. All this which is seen is not anything.

"Happiness beyond happiness" describes happiness beyond the typical happiness that comes from getting an object or situation you desired, or having an object or situation removed that you didn't like. That happiness quickly fades, followed by craving, longing, and disappointment and the endless self-referential internal narrative thoughts that go with them. The title of my first book, "Happiness Beyond Thought" describes that different type of happiness.

What "happiness" is not caused by thought, expectation, or imagining? What is "uncaused happiness", another title considered for that book? What is natural, persistent, happiness without a cause, without self-referential thoughts? That is the "happiness beyond happiness" that manifests in non-dual awakening.

As "akhilaa" translates as "complete" or "whole", and "adhaara" as "support" or "vehicle of Consciousness", this describes the all-pervading Self as the "basis of everything", and the complete "vehicle of Consciousness" that supports All that is.

WHAT IS THE TRANSCENDENTAL ILLUMINATING LIGHT?

aham	*eva*	*paraM*	*jyotiH*	*aham*	*eva*	*akhilaa*	*aatmakaH*
I am	alone	great	light	I am	alone	complete	Self

aanandaM	*paramaM*	*maanam*	*idaM*	*dRshyaM*	*na*	*kincana*
bliss	supreme	measure	all this	that is seen	is	nothing

I am, alone, the transcendental Light. I am, alone, the Self of all.
Bliss is the supreme measure. All this which is seen is not anything.

The famous Gaayatrii mantra is all about transcendental Light. Found in the Rig Veda, it is dedicated to the Sun deity and is widely cited in Vedic and post-Vedic texts including the Bhagavad Gita, Upanishads and the Buddhist Pali Canon. (1) (2) (3)

The Gaayatrii is an important part of the upanayana, rite-of-passage ceremony for young males in Hinduism. It has been recited by dvija, "twice born" spiritual men, as part of their daily rituals for millennia. Fortunately, Hindu reform movements extended the practice of the Gaayatrii to include women and all castes and its use is now widespread. (4)

The Gaayatrii is translated as:

> *We meditate on that eternal Reality as Light, which has no beginning and no end, which is the source of the highest wisdom and Truth.*

> *We meditate on the unchanging Reality as Light that bestows bliss and everlasting life and illuminates our intellect into the highest understanding.*

We meditate on that Light, which protects us from darkness and ignorance, and is the Light of all lights, the essence of everything, the One without a second, the bestower of immortality and everlasting peace.

That all-pervading Light is continually blessing us with enlightenment.

GARY WEBER PH.D.

HOW DOES ONE MOVE BEYOND THE EVERYDAY DANCE OF ENERGY?

aham	eva	hi	tRpta	atmaa	aham	eva	hi	nir	gunaH
I am	alone	truly	satisfied	Self	I am	alone	truly	without	gunas/attributes

aanandaM	paramaM	maanam	idaM	dRshyaM		na	kincana
bliss	supreme	measure	all this	that is seen		is	nothing

I am, alone, the satisfied Self. I am, alone, without attributes.
Bliss is the supreme measure. All this which is seen is not anything.

As described in earlier verses on thoughts and mind, gunas are an important concept in various philosophical schools across Samkhya and Hinduism. The most useful definition is "quality, attribute, property" and the three gunas are – *sattva* (knowledge, happiness), *rajas* (passion, attachment, desire) and *tamas* (inertia, laziness, ignorance, lack of discrimination) which "bind the immutable embodied being to the body".

Everyone has these three gunas in different degrees at different times, and is subject to their constant change and dance…unless they can "awaken", transcend and be beyond them. The entire 14th chapter of the Bhagavad Gita is concerned with how to transcend these gunas. As described in XIV, 5, such a person is called a "*guna-atiitaH*", or one who has transcended - *atiitaH* - the gunas.

To be "nirgunaH", or "without the gunas" is to not be moved by the dance of their energies and to be, as the first part of the verse indicates, the "satisfied Self".

The Bhagavad Gita in Chapter XIV, Verse 25 gives some guidelines for transcending the gunas and being a "guna-atiitaH":

maana	apamaanayoH	tulyaH	tulyaH	mitra	ari	pakshayoH
respect	disrespect	the same	the same	friend	enemy	their views

80

sarva	aarambhaH	parityaagii	gunaaH	atiitaH	saH	ucyate
all	undertakings	renounced	gunas	beyond	he	is called

(s)he who is the same whether (s)he is regarded with respect or disrespect, who has the same attitude towards the views of both friends and enemies, who has no sense of ownership or doership in undertakings – (s)he is said to have transcended the qualities/gunas (and become a guna-atiitaH). (1)

"Abandons the initiative in all undertakings" is often translated as "abandons all undertakings" or "given up all undertakings". The "abandons the initiative..." interpretation is the more useful one, preferred by Ramana Maharshi. It is better translated as "given up the desire for, and sense of doership/ownership of the results of all activities".

Ramana never encouraged anyone to abandon all undertakings or activities, but advised them to continue working where they were, and not retire to the cave or jungle, as the difficulties would only increase there. The key is to let go of one's *attachment* to the work, and do whatever it is that comes to you without feeling that it is MY work, which is the core of Karma Yoga.

Ramana, himself, was very active in "the undertakings" of the ashram, and heavily involved in daily meal preparations and construction. He and Annamalai Swami, the foreman for much of the expansion of the ashram, met every morning and evening to discuss the construction. (2)

CAN WE EVER FILL THAT "LACK", THAT "INCOMPLETENESS" THAT WE FEEL?

aham	eva	hi	puurna	atmaa	aham	eva	puraatanaH
I am	alone	truly	complete	Self	I am	alone	the ancient One

aanandaM	paramaM	maanam	idaM	dRshyaM	na	kincana
bliss	supreme	measure	all this	that is seen	is	nothing

I am, alone, the complete Self. I am alone the ancient One.
Bliss is the supreme measure. All this which is seen is not anything.

"Puurna" can also be translated as "perfectly full" to indicate that the Self is lacking nothing. One of the most useful descriptions of the state of abiding in the Self is "full emptiness" or "empty fullness".

A common feeling is that there is something missing, something lacking, that we try to somehow fill with all of our activities, diversions and pleasures. However, as we discover, our attempts fail and that great hollowness, that emptiness remains.

However, if we can deconstruct the ego/I, thoughts, mind and the belief that we are these bodies, this great "lack" is filled with total, complete, perfect fullness.

Similarly with being the "ancient One" which has always been here, and always will be, full and complete.

Can we reach a permanent, peaceful state?

aham	eva	hi	shaanta	atmaa	aham	eva	hi	shaashvataH
I am	alone	truly	peaceful	Self	I am	alone	truly	permanent

aanandaM	paramaM	maanam	idaM	dRshyaM	na	kincana
bliss	supreme	measure	all this	that is seen	is	nothing

I, alone, am the peaceful Self. I, alone, am permanent.
Bliss is the supreme measure. All this which is seen is not anything.

In Upadesa Saram, Verse 28, Ramana gives the answer:

kim	svaruupam	iti	aatma	darshane
what is	one's real nature	as to	the Self	the vision of

avyaya	abhava	aapuurna	cit	sukham
unending	unborn	all-pervading	Consciousness	Bliss

When one's real nature is found, and seen to be the Self, it is permanent, unborn, and all-pervading Consciousness-Bliss.

DOES THIS STATE EXTEND EVERYWHERE AND IS IT STABLE?

aham	eva	hi	sarvatra	aham	eva	hi	susthiraH
I am	alone	truly	everywhere	I am	alone	truly	stable

aanandaM	paramaM	maanam	idaM	dRshyaM	na	kincana
bliss	supreme	measure	all this	that is seen	is	nothing

I, alone, am everywhere. I, alone, am truly stable.
Bliss is the supreme measure. All this which is seen is not anything.

The term "susthiraH" is often translated as "well-established", which may connote having a great job, nice house, etc., so "truly stable" is used here. "Truly stable" is a strong statement, as where, in today's massively-complex world can a situation be found that exists everywhere and is truly stable? That distinguishes the Self as it is everywhere, is everything and is unchanging.

The Bhagavad Gita in Chapter XIII, Verse 27, gives a similar approach:

samam	sarveshu	bhuuteshu	tishthantam	parameshvaram
equally	in all	beings	residing	the Self

vinashyatsu	avinashyantam	yaH	pashyati	saH	pashyati
among the perishable	the imperishable	one	who sees	(s)he	sees

(S)he who sees the Self, residing equally in all beings – the imperishable among the perishable – the unchanging among the changing - sees clearly. (1)

Embark on a hunt for the Self. Keep looking for anything that does not change...mountains, oceans, rocks, trees, folk, plants, animals, earth, emotions, desires, fears, sensations, etc. Keep inquiring, "Does this change?" Something, something, doesn't change...

As mentioned earlier, it is easiest to see Her by looking between objects, breaths and thoughts rather than at them. Use the objects as pointers to where She is "unmanifested" as the Bhagavad Gita says. She is everywhere, but most obvious in the gaps and spaces.

The preceding 30 verses were those selected to cover the key issues involved in nondual awakening, but it didn't feel complete. It needed some closing, "capping" verses that didn't end with the "I am" section, which can feel "egoic" for some folk. Two verses were selected on "Knowledge of the Self", that met three criteria: a) Could they be easily learned?, b) Could they be chanted?, and c) Did they summarize the meaning of these texts and the entire Ribhu Gita? These are those verses.

KNOWLEDGE OF THE SELF

aatma	jnaanaM	paraM	shaastraM	aatma	jnaanam	anuupamaM
Self	knowledge	highest	science	Self	knowledge	unequalled

aatma	jnaanaM	paro	yoga	aatma	jnaanaM	paraa	gatiH
Self	knowledge	highest	yoga	Self	knowledge	supreme	goal

Knowledge of the Self is the supreme science. Knowledge of the Self is unequalled. Knowledge of the Self is the highest yoga. Knowledge of the Self is the supreme goal.

"anuupamaM" can also be translated as "beyond compare."

aatma	jnaanaM	cittana	ashaH	aatma	jnanaM	vimuktidaM
Self	knowledge	thought	termination	Self	knowledge	liberator

aatma	jnaanaM	bhyana	ashaM	atma	jnaanaM	sukha	avaham
Self	knowledge	fear	dispeller of	Self	knowledge	happiness	generator

Knowledge of the Self is the termination of thought. Knowledge of the Self is the liberator.
Knowledge of the Self is the dispeller of fear. Knowledge of the Self is the generator of happiness.

An important distinction is between "knowledge of the Self" and "self-knowledge". The spiritual marketplace is crowded with enthusiastic merchandisers of programs to know, understand, change, improve, modify, etc. your "self". However, knowledge of the Self is totally different. As these verses describe, it can a) end thought, b) liberate you from suffering, c) dispel your fears, and d) generate happiness. A comprehensive package is readily available, and free... you just have to do the practices.

The tradition of "capping verses" goes back to 10th century CE Zen, as an articulation, typically in verse, of Enlightenment – an experiential understanding of the nature of the world of "names and forms" and the Self.

Rinzai Zen is focused on solving kooans, paradoxical questions like "What is the sound of one hand clapping?" or "What was your face before your mother and father were born?". To demonstrate his/her insight, the monk brought a "capping phrase or verse" to the master for approval. Sometimes these "answers" were from one of the Zen phrase books compiled for this purpose, like *"Zen sand: the book of capping phrases for kōan practice"*, or *"A Zen Forest: Sayings of the Masters"*. (1) (2)

Interestingly, when the aspirant brought these "correct answers" to the master, they were typically rejected. The manner in which they were said revealed their lack of fully manifesting the experience.

It's like the story of a new arrival in a large group who being introduced around. The host would say "17", and everyone roared in laughter. Later the host said "34" and wild laughter ensued. The new arrival asked to try it. he said "17" and there was silence. The host replied, "well some can tell them and some can't." It's like that.

As my practice was the self-inquiry process of the 14th century CE Zen master, Bassui Tokushoo (3) and Ramana Maharshi, these "capping verses" come from the Ribhu Gita, one of Ramana's favorite texts.

It is indeed unequalled, the supreme science, the highest form of yoga, and the ultimate goal of the spiritual quest. Perhaps these 32 verses, learned, and chanted, again and again, and investigated with diligence and perseverance, can bring those same realities into "your" life.

The chants are available on my soundcloud channel and with mudras on my YouTube channel. (4) (5)

How does the software update process unfold in the real world?

The real questions on these updates to our software are a) Does it really work, b) How does someone "in the real world" do it with a "real job", and c) how does this process unfold?

The "Dialogues with Dominic" blog series looked at someone working in a financial management position in Chicago, with a growing family, and the challenges that go along with fitting an active self-inquiry practice into that situation. Those dialogues were so popular that they were made into a book, "Dialogues with Dominic: A Chronicle of Inquiry and Awakening" with Dominic Boyle as the author and Jake Yeager as the editor, which was published in 2016. It has been a very useful vehicle for many folk.

When this book manifested, the sequel series, "Dialogues with Oskar", felt like it would be a very useful addition. Oskar said that he would be proud to have it included in this book, so it is.

Oskar lives in Barcelona, Spain, is 45 years old and works as an IT Service Manager at Catalonia University. "K" as he prefers to be called, studied IT engineering for 5 years and is an avid rock climber and guide and sumi-e painter, is single and has meditated nearly every day for about 8 years.

These dialogues are from emails over 3+ years - oldest first. Most salutations and "thank yous" were removed, my responses are in italics. "K" is used throughout. The titles are the titles of the blogposts.

All sumi-e paintings are Oskar's manifestations and are included with his permission.

STRESSFUL SITUATIONS, ROCK CLIMBING, LONELINESS, ISOLATION

G

Hi Oskar,

Great that you found the article in Liberation Unleashed useful. Feel free to translate into Spanish and post it wherever you like.

K

I've been reading your blog for a while and I find it amazing. The relation between awakening and science is something I was lacking for a long time being quite rational. Also I'm glad to find practical steps outside of religion and tradition to see through the illusion of separate self.

Yesterday I bought your book and started reading it.

I've never been in the presence of an awakened being. I don't expect anything magical but people used to say that being in the presence of one and talking to him/her is useful for gaining confidence in the process.

Do you know of anyone enlightened in Spain or Catalonia? I must say that I'm not very confident about the state of awakening of lots of yoga gurus and Zen masters around here... :(

G

If you are meant to be "in the presence of an awakened being", it will occur, as will whether it really makes any difference. Many folk went to see Ramana Maharshi; some were transformed, others felt "something", others felt "nothing" and saw only an old man in a loincloth lying on a couch.

There are many un-awakened yoga gurus and Zen masters; your caution is well-advised. Some are outright charlatans and are very successful and popular - it is surprisingly easy if one changes their hair, clothes and how they speak, to fool many folk. Others are perhaps well-intentioned, but have no real experience of what they are saying.

The best way to find one of these folk is to do your practices as diligently as you can. As the saying goes, "When the student is ready, the teacher will appear". your teacher might not even manifest "physically". my main teacher, Ramana Maharshi, had passed before i was old enough to see him, but he is more real to me than any "live" person.

K

I will follow your advice: keep my practices and let life unfold.

you've been very helpful.

Yesterday I felt very alone in a dream, feeling everyone being robots without self but with me still a person. i couldn't get rid of the illusion, so I was seeing the world empty and unfolding but couldn't free myself. Everything was ONE and without self except for me. So I was alone in the universe and felt very, very lonely.

But I accept that dream as a good premonition :)

G

That is a prescient dream as to what it can feel like.

The sense of being lonely comes and goes, and as time goes on, and the brain stabilized the new functional pattern more and more, the feeling goes away and it is a very sweet space.

you may also feel everything "within you", which amounts to the same thing. The dream was not just a premonition, it is what awakening can feel like at first.

K

you mention rock climbing in your book. i've been rock climbing for more than fifteen years and last month I was climbing in Kentucky (Red River Gorge) for two weeks.

I'm not sure why but lots of rock climbers have a tendency to mysticism. It could be because you face the possibility of death often and see clearly how many things in life are really not that important, or it could be because when you climb, you experience very clearly, no-self moments.

I have the hypothesis that when your life is in danger, your body switches-off the non-vital systems to focus completely on the problem, and the ego goes away in that process...

After some minutes it always comes back. But sometimes you reach the ground after climbing and then think "uau! I wasn't there for some minutes, my body just did what was needed alone, and it did really well!!!"

No thoughts, just action, perfect action, some call it "flow". I wasn't aware of that till I was a bit more mature in my meditation.

G

i'm not a rock climber, but my younger daughter is, and one of my long term folk is a dedicated climber, caver and skier.

It is a great way to achieve "stillness" w/the complete focus on the task at hand, knowing that if you lose concentration the consequences can be very severe. As you saw, "you weren't there" and your "body did just what was needed alone, and it did very well!!!" (The blogpost "Are our lives controlled by our unconscious brain" discusses this in rock climbing.)

"Flow" is experienced by elite athletes, chess grandmasters, artists, teachers, etc. as well as climbers. Mihaly Csikszentmihalyi's book "Flow" was a great "study" of the phenomena. your whole life can be that way if you just "aren't there". (1)

K

I think that as I'm lacking the presence of a master, sensei or guru, that this emailing could help me to fill that loss. Books and blogs do the same function and for me they are a great motivation, while trying to be very selective and not believing everything I read.

My practice is mainly trying to do formal meditation abiding in the I-sense, mostly following Ed Mujika's and Rajiv Kapur's instructions and trying to keep my awareness, and self-questioning the rest of the day, turning back to that silent presence every time I recall the need to do so, and trying to be aware of feelings and thoughts as they arise.

Am seeing how useless thoughts are, and thinking intellectually that the "I" has no scientific proof of existence.

When I was climbing for two weeks, I couldn't meditate much. I'm finding it very difficult to meditate again like my body or ego doesn't want to do so, but in daily life I'm feeling more and more focused, alert and aware. It's strange.

I'm seeing clearer and clearer when thoughts and feelings arise, and I pass some time in silent awareness even while working, driving, at meetings, having a tea...

I can now feel how my mind generates a motivation for doing something. It's felt without words, impossible to explain, but I feel it, and how then my "I" says inside my head the same thing that my mind-body-self was going to do, repeating like a parrot something that is not HIS idea but an idea coming from the subconscious.

It's amazing, it's very subtle and I'm not able to feel it always. It happens very fast of course, in less than a second. But, even though I knew this is how it works I didn't expect to be able to feel it! To see it!

G

i don't know Ed Mujika's or Rajiv Kapur's teaching, so couldn't comment on that. What you describe sounds excellent especially the "rest of the day" work on self-inquiry.

What you describe as sitting meditation being "worse" and the other 15 hours being "better", is the target we're aiming at. This work isn't about improving your meditations, it is about making your daily living better. Excellent work is likely occurring in both meditation and moment-to-moment during the day, "off line".

your "seeing clearer and clearer..." is excellent. That is exactly as it proceeds, naturally, and "normally". you're doing really well.

K

Your positive feedback is helping me a lot as are your blog and articles. Another great factor motivating me is that I always felt a bit out of the religious-thing, more agnostic than Buddhist or Advaitic.

You say it is about making your moment-to-moment living better. Now I feel at peace most of the time even now that my life is going through some stressful situations (changing my home next month, a relationship I think I have to end, lots of friends with economic problems...). I should feel bothered but I don't.

I'm not yet able to feel that no matter what happens it will be OK, but I'm able to wait in peace and see what happens without worrying much. It has little to do with ME because there's no me to worry about. I just don't think much about past or future now...

It's funny that these changes in daily life happen so slowly that I wasn't even aware of them until I start thinking about it. I wasn't aware that day after day I'm taking life more like flowing with the Tao... :)

Sometimes I get a little stressed again for a while, but these moments are fewer and fewer...Now, I feel that the main thing I want to do is keep up my practice, and all the rest is felt like secondary right now. It's sometimes a bit worrying too... :)

G

It is for situations just like yours that this work is so useful and important. Realizing that whatever happens is just what happens, and is out of your control, is the best and most effective possible action one can take.

If you are fully present, and not lost in thoughts, worries and stories that do nothing positive but take you out of the moment and "into your head", you can be much more "useful" to others and to yourself.

Being fully present, in the "now, now, now", and moving in the flow of the Dao/ Tao, even for your relationship that may be dancing its way to its end, and the economic distress that your friends, region, and country are experiencing, is the best and most powerful action that can be taken for them and for "you".

K

While I write this I'm feeling a soft peace that is with me most of the time now. I think my practice is moving in good direction.

Every day that passes I'm more sure that awakening is really possible and I see a bit clearer how the process is unfolding, how thoughts get weaker or felt as not important, just redundant and disturbing.

Awareness, peace and some detachment from the world arises slowly...

GARY WEBER PH.D.

CONSCIOUSNESS, RESISTANCE, SPIRITUAL IDENTITY, PROGRESS

K

Is all this just a training game for the brain to change or is there something beyond that? Something beyond the material world and the laws of physics?

G

Yes, there is "Something" beyond that, IME, encompasses all of us, is in and through all of us. Our latest quantum physics and cosmology points to the reality of this Universal Field, but they can only go so far.

As the field must have at least all of the properties we have, and as it is pervasive, it is likely self-aware, self-conscious, and learning about itself. (2)

Much occurs in my daily life that is highly improbable and very synchronistic - this is the most logical explanation, IMHO. If one accepts this, then one surrenders to the Universal Field, which has been running everything all along anyway, beyond our cognition or control.

K

Thank you very much :)

I found it interesting that you like chanting and music. Someone said that if you give some practices to the mind that it likes (like music or the bliss of presence), it lets the process unfold without interfering much.

Does it make sense?

G

Agree that giving the mind something to be interested in, like chanting, can help the process unfold w/o interfering. However, Presence is not giving the mind something to do.

Presence has always been there, and is seen naturally, as mind gets out of the way. The less of I/me/my there is, the less "mind" there is, until all there is, is Presence.

K

Experiencing some problems in meditating, like my body or mind doesn't want to do it, but the rest of the day I felt more focused than ever. Yesterday I felt very sad and depressed. I'm a happy person and don't feel that way often. I couldn't find any reason for my sadness.

After lunch I took a break and suddenly felt that *thoughts are leading my life and I don't have any control over them*, so I don't have any control in my life. I knew it before, but somehow I felt it more deeply this time. I felt really detached from my thoughts and was really sure that life unfolds without my doing...

The rest of the day passed very happily with fewer thoughts than ever and a good sensation of Presence and bliss. In some moments, I even thought that It was going to last forever.

Today I feel more like always but I can connect to my feeling of Presence more easily than ever and somehow I feel more peaceful. This morning I couldn't meditate well. It was like my sense of "I am" was too weak...

It was like a very, very small kensho. I'm feeling very optimistic!

Thank you for all.

K

I've kept working and the process keeps unfolding. Meditation is deeper than ever and quite effortless. In the past weeks, there are lots of days in which I feel that thoughts appear and disappear without touching "me".

In meditation some days, there are lots of thoughts but it's as if *they aren't mine.* They don't disturb me most of the time, they're just irrelevant, and I ignore them.

Abiding in my Self is quite continuous now. It all started about one month ago after some kind of insight I had about the nature of myself as awareness - first about awareness being present all the time and second about relaxing into no-doership.

I cannot say it's absolutely stable, but I feel that now I'm really starting to abide in my real Self, most of the time. Sometimes, I get lost in *powerful thoughts (mostly spiritual ones)* but they're few.

Personal events happen now that earlier could affect me, but I see them as just "what it is". I'm not perfectly at peace and relaxed but I'm not worried or anxious either.

I keep working, but now it doesn't feel like working. I feel good even when I cannot meditate because of time pressures. It worried me a lot some months ago, but now I feel that the whole day, the whole life, is practice in itself.

Thank you very much for all, amigo.

G

The fact that your meditation is now deeper and effortless and that you have had deep insights on the "the nature of myself as awareness" is excellent.

Having most of your problematic thoughts be about "spiritual" work is what can easily happen.

It is a challenge to not get caught up in our "spiritual identity", particularly as we see more progress and the experiences deepen.

The best antidote is to recognize that our spiritual identity, is just that, another identity, and no more wonderful or useful than any other identity.

Many folk get lost here, and their "spiritual" achievement fades, as it only manifested when the "I", spiritual or not, was not there. The "I" is always anxious to rush in and claim credit for any achievement, including spiritual ones, which it had no part in creating.

Keep doing your practice, alert for the I/ego deflecting deeper work, like blocking a particular inquiry. Shifting from "Where am I?", or "When am I?" to an affirmation or negation, like "I am not this body", "I am not these thoughts", etc. can continue to move the practice deeper.

Move the practice into your daily interactions w/others as they are where we will see ourselves most clearly. This is really important if you don't have time to do your meditation practice. Constant watchfulness is the price of freedom.

Persist, persist, persist.

K

While going to sleep I was trying to see clearly that I'm not my thoughts and felt a very subtle shift in identification. In the past 'my' thoughts were telling me "you're consciousness", but no one was really believing.

I felt that for the first time *I was Consciousness and not thoughts. There was no doubt.* Some subtle but important change was made in identification or beliefs. All thoughts are seen as unimportant and useless as they arise, but are pervaded by a great silence and calm.

Old feelings and identification returned, very subtle, less strong, but they persist. I go back to peaceful consciousness automatically after every thought or text read or spoken. I felt that was an important kensho.

Thank you very much, how can I thank you for all the help you're giving me?

G

Yes, that is just how it is, just a subtle shift, but a vast change. One moment, you are your thoughts trying to understand how you can be Consciousness...the next moment, it shifts and you clearly are, and always have been, and will always be, Consciousness.

Thoughts are manifesting, but they aren't "you". It is so clear, so evident, so right, so "yes".

A deep pervasive Stillness is there, naturally, easily, and softly. Even as thoughts arise and fall away, less frequently than before, they aren't identified with, aren't who you are. They're just like the mist passing through the mountains, owned by no one.

K

Should I keep practicing as before or change something?

Meditation now is like doing nothing, the real shikantaza - just abiding in me. It doesn't really matter if there are thoughts or not... and of course that helps to go deeper...

Somehow I feel that my daily mindfulness is worse than before but I think it's just a feeling because no effort is made in any moment to go back to awareness, to me...

Love

G

Feel your way into the "right" balance between a) allowing the brain to deconstruct the "I" itself, while "you" are passive and b) engaging a "mini-doer" to actively deconstruct the residue of the "I", which is still there.

If there are self-referential thoughts, there is an I/me/my there, and it will adapt to the new situation and reassert itself. Continue w/a) until it is obvious that there is increasing obscuring of the "Stillness".

The perception that "daily mindfulness is worse than before" is not a good indicator, as our memories of prior states are incorrect and heavily influenced by how we feel now. The blogpost - "Traumatic memories feel true, but are always changing" discusses this. (3)

As you have gotten more still, what before were minor, or unnoticed phenomena, now seem much larger. It gets more and more subtle.

K

Yes, there's still work to do! :)

Keeping meditating, and some kind of mini-doer, during the rest of the day sounds perfect to me!

I'm not sure what you mean by "increasing obscuring of the stillness".

G

By "increasing obscuring of stillness", i mean that you should continue "passively" until you see that "Stillness", which is always present, starts to be clouded over by the I/ego. When you do, "actively" engage the "mini-doer" with some inquiry to clear away the clouds again and see only the Stillness.

K

It's been about a month and a half since my last mail.

I've been enjoying a new life. First I was amazed and then sometimes I was in an "I got it/I lost it" anguish until I saw that it was impossible to "lose it" :)

Stillness and silence are getting deeper and the sense of an Oskar is getting very weak. All thoughts are weak and their impact in the body or mind doesn't last.

NEW PLACES, LOSING CONTROL, FEWER OSKARS, LOVE...

K

I was climbing in China. In the past progress is great while on holidays or out of "my usual world" and this was also the case.

I've kept doing formal meditation but in daily activities it is hard to not "forget myself", as in "not being aware of awareness". I don't feel it is needed. My mini-doer is very weak now and I live most of the time just letting things happen, no past, no future.

I've been focusing on non-duality, and "Where am I?" comes to mind often. I'm starting to look to the world trying to deepen its nonduality…it's difficult to explain. I don't feel the seen world as "me" but I feel attracted by my perceptions to show me something.

The sense of self is losing its position, so it's hard to say "where" I am.

G

Being out of our "usual world" is a great place for major progress. In our "usual world", there are many "memory tags" that pull us into stories. In a new environment, the brain is more alert and focused, and w/o "tags", deeper work is possible.

The state you are in is not a problem. As you have seen, it is impossible to "lose it", which is a great understanding. The "I" is becoming dissociated as it is apparent that there is no solid, fundamental, singular "I". The individual "I"s are becoming smaller, but not uniformly…some faster, others slower.

It will become apparent that "the brain is driving the bus" and that you aren't in control of what is happening. The brain is rearranging its neural structure to abide in that Stillness which it wants above all else.

The brain has always reorganized "by itself". It re-functionalizes to improve skills in rock climbing, writing code, doing IT tasks, learning another language, etc., as it adapts to new skills or environments.

Now, it is re-functionalizing the I/me/my construct. The more "data" it gets from glimpses of stillness, the faster it will stabilize in its desired state, returning "Home".

Feeling that you don't need to do formal meditation is typical. The residue of the "I" runs around saying "I MUST DO SOMETHING". Feel carefully if DOING SOMETHING is not "right" - not "in balance". Trust that deep intuition. The "I" is panicking, trying to justify its existence.

Things are going well. Relax, abide, be as still as possible.

If "Where am I?" is manifesting, go with that. Use your perceptions as pointers to what is perceiving - don't get distracted. Imagine yourself on the object and look back at what is perceiving.

K

Your words always resonate with me. It's always like a Christmas gift to receive your mail :)

The path seems easy, but it's subtle. Let's see how I let the brain do all the work. As you said, the feeling of "me" is getting weaker as awareness grows.

I'm meditating now but because I found it peaceful and joyful. I'm moving from the concentration of shikantaza to "just being well with myself", aligned with your advice.

It's happening by/for itself. I never thought about doing it before it happened. All things happen this way :)

I'll follow your great advice: be still, be calm, relax

A T-shirt says "stay at the center and let all the things take their course - Lao Tse" :)

K

It's like you said. The brain/mind is doing the work all alone and Oskar is getting more transparent day after day.

I keep sitting just when it is "wanted". Just sitting in every moment, doing nothing but staying with myself.

Enjoying roller skating for kms without thinking much. After the workout, the stillness is even greater than after meditating! :)

Beginning sumi-e classes. So nice to paint with an empty mind.

Thank you again for all dear Gary

G

Such a beautiful flowering, like sumi-e, roller skating without thinking, and sitting in stillness - "doing nothing but staying with myself".

So simple, and yet so elegant, this work is.

K

It's been some time since my last mail :) I don't like talking about myself as I feel like everything I say isn't really truthful.

Something changes slowly day after day. There are highs and lows but there's always progress…

The feeling of not being in charge of anything is very strong. I feel some impersonality, like being lived or sometimes feeling like every moment is a now-now-now. No plans, no past…just let happen what has to happen (and enjoy the show).

Thoughts haven't totally stopped, but they're quite irrelevant. They happen as background.

Me is not at any location. It's like looking at reality from outside the world, not exactly with my eyes. Consciousness is not located at any concrete point.

Perceptions are brighter and closer, sounds brighter, clearer and louder. I perceive some subtle change in perception but it's difficult to define.

Most of the time I really feel no one is here, just awareness. Sometimes that makes me feel a bit worried that I haven't been present enough. But not much. :)

Past-I is nearly over - like I don't have a past. :) It's there but never recalled. Future-I is less deconstructed, but very weak. I can still get disturbed with problems.

Most of the time I feel peace and stillness.

Meditation is deeper every day. Sitting and looking, waiting for whatever has to arise. I'm getting close to something like a "zero" state. No reason for that, no big deal. I meditate just because. I'm not in charge anyway. :) I meditate as any other activity, just because it has to be done. :)

G

Great that perceptions are changing and that you are having a difficult time pin-pointing where you are. What remains of the Oskars will suggest approaches to be "done" to make things "better".

"...the feeling of not being in charge of anything is very strong", as well as feeling you're "being lived" in "now, now, now" are strong indicators that the brain has taken over the process. The pattern is being worked out as it "cuts and tries" to optimize and strengthen the new modified OS.

Just keep "sitting and looking" in peace and stillness, not knowing why you're do-ing the "meditation". This is valuable "data time" for the brain w/o narrative mind interference.

Trying to guess how things are going from the conscious mind's vantage point is futile. It can't see the "unconscious", which is why it's called that. It's like trying to understand how a clock works by watching it tell time. It is great that "we" can't be aware of, and involved in, what the brain is doing, because we would almost certainly mess it up.

Being disturbed by problems will diminish. Watch for narrative spinning a big story. If that occurs, engage the surrender/letting go approaches or just simply "let go, let go" of it.

It is going "beautifully" Oskar, or whatever remains of that fellow...

K

After six months living in that new world, while roller-skating it was suddenly realized that "I'm just LIFE" – that brought me a lot of energy and happiness that still lasts. It was a very energetic feeling of being alive, just life!

It wasn't denying that I was consciousness but somehow it was added to consciousness. It was related to energy and feeling – before it was all thought and consciousness.

It's hard to describe.

It's obvious that we're life, but it's very clear now that I feel bliss and love more often, more like I'm consciousness-bliss or awareness-life.

I feel more focused and alive with fewer thoughts and am less identified with them. They arise and pass without any trace.

Whatever I am remains just being there, while body and mind do their work. Recently there was some tension about thoughts that now has disappeared and I feel more stable and at peace.

I had a dream. Feeling a lot of love, love as I've never felt, and opening my eyes, my love was all over the things I see, over all the world, and the world was also me, everything was me and was love. It was very intense.

FEWER THOUGHTS, VERY STILL, 2D/3D PERCEPTIONS, NO DOERSHIP

G

Things are going "perfectly" with your reported changes:

    a)   *thoughts and consciousness > feeling deep happiness,*

    b)   *more consciousness-bliss and awareness with fewer, and decreased attachment to, self-referential thoughts,*

    c)   *increased stability and peace*

    d)   *seeing love over everything*

This is real progress which will continue and become more stable. The brain has identified the state that it wants and is refining the neural networks, clearing out unwanted memories and disassembling the egoic/I construct.

As this proceeds, you will observe great states, but they may be followed by periods of confusion. This is typical as the brain is "carrying away the trash" from the reconstruction.

The brain is likely working in an orderly fashion. However, "consciousness" sees this alternating pattern of stillness, stability, love, peace, etc. and a jangled, disordered state.

In your "knowledge" work, planning and problem-solving thoughts carrying out those functions are "fine" - they are not emotionally-loaded, or problematic and are not touched by the process.

If self-referential narrative, emotionally-loaded thoughts arise, use self-inquiry or "let go, let go". This will develop into a heuristic, an "algorithm", for these problem types, which is automatically invoked, and removes them almost before they can be observed.

Enjoy the dance.

K

Hi again, dear Sensei so-far-away :)

Things are going on as you said. I'm so thankful for your help that I hope that someday I could help you in any way or do something for you. Let me know if the moment arises... whatever...

Self-referential thought is nearly over. Practical thought happens when it's needed but not about a supposed Oskar. Some events can upset me for a short moment...but they don't last. I let things flow and deepen. Most of the time there's only stillness.

When a thought about the old-I arises, I feel un-ease almost immediately. My body doesn't want an "I"!!! It's rejecting even the thought of it!

Perception keeps changing. Not only are things brighter and closer, but also their quality is changing. Sometimes they feel more 3D than ever and sometimes it's like a painting. Will I feel sometime that all I see is One with me? I'm starting to believe it. :)

My mind is disturbing "me" about whether I should "force" attention or just let go absolutely, letting go of attention... What do you think?

I can be "out-of-this-world" and my body keeps doing and thinking, with no clear "me" and no attention at all for some time. Or i can force myself to be present and aware of everything, happy and blissful, but it feels artificial.

Probably the answer is to let go of that doubt and let my body-mind do the re-programming work in peace…isn't it?

Could I send you an original painting? It would be an expression of my love for you.

G

Don't be concerned that "some events can upset me for a short moment". That is difficult to stop. Sometimes it is a fast basic response to a situation that the brain evolved to regard as likely dangerous. Others are just long-conditioned responses. The blogpost "How do i deal with anger? i can't meditate it away" may be useful. (4)

The important thing is that they "don't last", as you are finding. That is where an emotion generates a story with destructive narrative. It sounds as if you have moved beyond that.

The "unease" when the old "I" tries to manifest is typical as one progresses. The brain prefers the stillness and Now so it creates a "drug enhancement" process to stay in that space. As Ramana Maharshi said, "It will become difficult to even manifest thought". The blogpost "Do drugs, sex, competition and meditation use the same "pleasure" system" describes this. (5)

your perceptions will continue to have this shifting from 2-D to 3-D phenomena. you may find you will be able to consciously shift back and forth between them, like with one of those visual puzzles where it is either a vase, or two people facing each other.

"All is One" will emerge, unexpectedly. Don't force it, it will just be there, and then fade away. you will be left knowing that is the Truth, always. It will increasingly be felt, at some level, all the time.

As far as "forcing" yourself to be present, you have the answer with your "let go of that doubt and let my body-mind do the re-programming work". you felt that the forced situation was "more artificial".

Only a faint sense of the "I" remains to raise those concerns.

It would be great to have one of your sumi-e paintings.

Wonderful work, here Oskar, wonderful

K

You're great, Sensei.

Your statement *"your perceptions will continue to have this shifting from this 2-D to 3-D phenomena. you may find you will be able to consciously shift back and forth between them, like with one of those visual puzzles where it is either a vase, or two people facing each other"* is exactly what is happening. I can shift consciously.

I was very lucky finding your blog... and then you :)

K

As you said, things keep deepening, and now "no effort" is clearer than ever.

I'm starting to feel very light - Oskar is really disappearing slowly.

Meditation is effortless and deeper than ever. It really doesn't matter if there are thoughts or not. They as less and less present. I see clearly that the thought-process is just a question of clinging. If you don't attach to things and events, thoughts relax... But they're not a problem anyway, no more...

The feeling of non-doership is growing. Everything gets done spontaneously in the "now", with no need to worry. Strong feelings are even less problematic. Just life unfolding. Just touching the surface of my consciousness.

There are no stories about a "me" and thoughts are mainly future plans - very operational ones.

The bliss now is present more than ever, just relaxing and observing.

Subtle changes in perceptions keep coming and going. I'm starting to forget about practice or progress, but I don't worry much about it. Sometimes I'm inside perception, inside scenery (and not behind) and sometimes there's no difference between inside and outside, no distance at all.

The presence of a thought pretending to be Oskar, very rare nowadays, clearly blocks bliss and that kind of perception when it happens.

G

Unfolding is manifesting perfectly and naturally w/o effort or "doer", just like the famous Soto Zen poem: Sitting quietly, doing nothing, spring comes and the grass grows, by itself.

Wonderful stuff...

K

I was reading a comment in your last blogpost: "'blah, blah' – understanding its contents and effects...recent research". (6)

"In effect, she is saying that there are multiple layers of self-referencing (experiential with neural correlates), of varying intensities, that separate dual and non-dual experience. In your particular case, all the layers ceased simultaneously. As you point out, there may be other ways to "skin the cat" as well."

That's my case right now. As you said, as I keep my practice and keep living, my brain seems to be re-programming in an organic way how it works. Every few weeks it feels like something is missing in reference to self-referential thoughts.

There are subtle changes quite often, no big bangs, or new kenshos, but subtle changes. Lots of changes are hard to describe, others are clear, like no wandering thoughts about past or myself, no sensation of time, etc.

Non-dual luminosity in seeing is very present most of the time, as is that strange property of vision like I'm more inside the scenery. I'm sure you know what I mean.

Stillness is also growing (and bliss). A new state that is very, very, still, and very, very silent is starting to appear from time to time for a short moment.

Conscious thinking is more and more detached from identifying with a "me". Thoughts come and go when stillness is lost but they are no problem at all, not at all. No need to even see them as false, no need to do anything right now, they're really "blah, blah, blah".

The sensation of non-doership is growing - feeling life flow, flowing with the Tao, sitting as a passenger and enjoying a blissful nice travel...

NON-DUAL SEEING, "I" BLOCKER, BLISS, LIBERATION, JUST "NOW"

G

The process is proceeding "perfectly". "Letting go" keeps what is left of the various Oskars from trying to come back in and stop anything. If one manifested as a "doer" to make something "better", that would feel "not OK" now, so it would fall away naturally.

The brain is "driving the bus", and recognizes what needs to be done. The growing bliss, stillness and intermittent arrival of a very, very still state are indications of the progress it is making.

Remember that the brain is likely at work almost continuously on this new OS during the day on this as well as its regular jobs, trying iteration after iteration to see what works best, and then during sleeping is hauling away the debris from all of the reconstructive work.

The blogpost "Why do we sleep? Evolutionary mistake? Catch-up napping" gives the latest science on the cleanup and housekeeping the brain does while we sleep. (7)

It is like building a new highway, space needs to be cleared away for the new route. It is constructed and tried for a while, until some new route is indicated, and more work is done.

K

An interesting shift happened.

I was able to perceive the subtle thought that builds the idea of a "me" looking for something. It's just a shadow of an intention. It was realized that true "seeing" is always non-dual. There is that subtle mental construction acting as an observer, a "me", that is the real duality.

The perception switched to "non-dual" in a more stable way that keeps going on, always bright and at the same time absolutely close to me, but very alive. The sense of "me" as that subtle thought dropped away some hours later and more bliss is felt as a natural situation now.

Could be a minor change in the OS has been uploaded :)

G

An excellent understanding, seeing the "I" attempting to arise, but being unable to pop up. Perhaps a pop-up blocker "uploaded" that blocks the "I". If it does arise, the blocker shuts it down again.

Important to realize that this is a subroutine. As the OS improves, the pop-up may be eliminated, or become just a "click on" app.

Great progress.

K

Everything keeps evolving to a new way of being...the transparent subject is dissolving into nothing, into scenery and universe.

Bliss is appearing very often, for no reason, just for being alive, sometimes subtle, sometimes quite strong. Love is growing, stillness is growing.

Perception is non-dual whenever attention is focused. Thoughts are not a problem. They're just "nonsense talking" and are decreasing and decreasing.

The degree of non-duality is variable. Sometimes it's luminosity without labelling, but other times it's deeper. I'm starting to really feel I am the outer world, with nothing inside.

The mystery keeps growing. Sometimes I feel like I'm sinking into no-thingness and no-knowledge. Who am I? It's more mystery than ever, but I don't much care :)

Just keep flowing with attention on...

G

Everything is going very well.

The great Presence is absorbing what's left of the I/me/my avatar, organically and naturally. As you are "sinking into no-thingness and no-knowledge", you will find that your functional competency will not decrease.

The apparent varying of nonduality is the brain refining its networks. As it adjusts and improves, the state will become more stable and energy efficient, just like when one learns to ride a bicycle, write computer programs or rock climb.

The brain loves the Stillness, Presence and peace. It will continue to improve and use its dopamine reward/pleasure system to ensure that this state is so pleasurable and compelling that there will be no interest in moving out of it.

Just keep letting go, letting go, letting go...

K

Changes are happening quite fast.

Most of my time I'm seeing that luminosity or non-dual seeing, like the world is bright and absolutely intimate to me.

Thought is present sometimes and sometimes not. It has lost some quality. Thought is now never about a "me" - it has lost all of its self-referential quality. I'm absolutely untouched by them. Even if the thought is saying something about "me", all its power is gone.

Every negative sensation lasts for a really, really short time and leaves without traces and without importance.

I really feel I could finally say with conviction that "no one is really here". It's not an absence but a flowing and ever changing presence without any center.

Meditation is no more meditation, it's just sitting and being like the rest of the day but more focused and silent - little difference really. I keep doing it because it feels right...

Most of this is thanks to you, thank you.

G

Wonderful...it is now doing it all by itself. There is nothing that needs to be done, or anyone left to do it.

What a great surprise to have your fantastic, incredibly "Zennish" art work arrive today. It really captures the essence of stillness and the preciousness of this very moment, just now, and now, and now... It is "present" on my desk...looking like it has found its place...

Many gasshos for your thoughtfulness and creativity.

K

I feel so happy and blissful now, Gary. I sent you all my love and peace with the painting.

As you said there seems to be no end to letting go and peace...

For me you always will be part of my path, thank you, thank you :)

K

For Catalonia and Spain these are times of change. It's quite hard for some people, but there's happiness from inside from the love for them. I can cry but feel OK at the same time, because this crying is also an expression of love.

G

There are so many great difficulties all across Europe now, and in the Middle East.

As you say, "crying is also an expression of love". The great value of this work is to recognize that while we have no control over the external circumstances of our lives, we can have a great inner stillness, peace and love that is untouched.

At such times, those tears are not only tears of love, but of joy, surrender, and gratitude.

K

Hi, Sensei.

You're right, there's no end to the dissolution of the subject. Day after day there's less "I" here as you learn how to let go of deeper and deeper layers of mind, subtler and subtler.

The changes in the brightness and quality of perception are amazing - very, very bright and alive with no inside, no outside, just it. The world's there, but not there. you let go of perception, abandon the world and you're in another dimension, just being... or simply you are not.

It seems impossible to attach any craving or anger to a self even for minutes...no subject, no suffering, nothing to get attached to, no stories, no tales.

Thoughts nearly gone, just some random ones here and there while working in the world. It's magic how can you function in the world, transparent but better than before.

Gratitude to reality in the form of G. Weber. Thank you :)

G

Yes, it is exactly as you describe, magnificent in how it all dances so perfectly, so exquisitely down to the finest detail. Just totally surrender, and then you are totally held. Everything happens perfectly, "all by itself".

What manifests may not always at first appear to be a "good" thing, but if one watches carefully, it is clear why it happened. It always leads to deepening the understanding, moving further into the stillness. Just when you "thought" it couldn't get any deeper, any more "locked down", it does exactly that.

K

Dear Sensei,

After awakening it was clear that it wasn't liberation, but now, after two and a half years of surrender, bliss is nearly always present, and thought is totally self-liberated every moment.

Even events that in the past were a big drama, now are provoking just some seconds of physical reaction. Life is just this now…no thoughts of future of past, no need for them. Just this present-bliss-universe, even for a knowledge worker like this IT engineer.

Love and compassion arise out of nowhere. When you have "nothing to do", when you "abandon every wish and rejection", what else is worth doing except helping others?

The universe is so close, that it's me. It feels absolutely intimate. "Me" has been spread all over reality.

Thank you :)

Love

The greatest resistance to changing the software - "Free Will"

Nothing is so fundamental to nondual awakening, nor as strongly resisted as the understanding of having no "free will". Folk have shouted in my face, said that someone would kill me, etc. over their strong belief in having "free will". Possessing "free will" is at the heart of most religions, judicial systems, institutions, cultures and marketing. Contemporary neuroscience, virtually all mystical traditions and my own personal experience demonstrate just the opposite, that we have no such "free will" or "control". Our (apparent) decisions are made without consulting our "conscious" ego/I, and our actions manifest seamlessly without our conscious involvement.

The perspectives of the premier scientist and the premier sage of the 20th century CE are strikingly similar on this topic:

Albert Einstein:
"Everything is determined, the beginning as well as the end, by forces over which we have no control. It is determined for

insects as well as for the stars. Human beings, vegetables, or cosmic dust, we all dance to a mysterious tune, intoned in the distance by an invisible piper."

"You can will what you want, but you can't will what you will". (1)

Ramana Maharshi:

Q. "Are only the important events in a man's life, such as his main occupation or profession, predetermined, or are trifling acts also, such as taking a cup of water or moving from one part of the room to another?"

RM: "Everything is predetermined." (2)

Blogposts on the topic, not surprisingly, draw much interest and conflict. This section of the book contains comments on those blogposts with editing only for brevity without sacrificing meaning and some spelling and grammatical corrections. Deletions are marked by "...". my responses to comments are italicized. Each blogpost is broken out separately. Similar questions and responses and personal comments were not used. Many similar comments and responses on the "free will", control, and predetermination videos are on my youTube channel.

There's no free will...accept it, attack it, hide it or ignore it?

Sean:

Does there need to be a free will / determinism dichotomy in philosophy? Just as free will has been proven inconsistent with science, so has determinism. The double slit experiment shows that the present state of a quantum particle may lead to a spectrum of future states, each with a particular likelihood of occurring. Bringing this to the macroscopic level, perfect knowledge of a person's neuroanatomy would not allow determination of their actions perfectly. In the context of nonduality, this understanding seems to provide another level of freedom, surrender, mystery, spontaneity, etc.

Gary:

Hi Sean. The uncertainty principle of quantum mechanics can't be impacted by your "free will", unless you are personally choosing how to collapse all of those wave functions in your body as you choose. There are approximately 7 X 10 to the 27th power or 7,000,000,000,000,000,000,000,000,000 atoms in a 150 lb. human body.

As quantum mechanics only works for sub-atomic particles, the actual number of quantum events in your body is much, much higher than this. you have no ability to be aware of, nor simultaneously arrange over 7 billion, billion, billion events.

Knowing perfectly all of the neuroanatomy and neurochemistry in your own body, so that "you" could exercise "free will" on that is similarly daunting. There are approximately 100 billion neurons and about 50 trillion or so synaptic connections in your body so it would be similarly impossible.

The point of Dr. Steven Cave's comment is that if all of that could be known, as it does totally dictate your responses, your behavior could be predicted perfectly. To have personal "free will", you would have to be able to control, manipulate and manage all of that, which you couldn't do.

Also, in order to know and choose between two possibilities with any meaning, you would have to know what their ultimate outcomes would be, as those choices worked their way through space time interacting with countless others, which is similarly unknowable.

As "you" can't know, or control your neurochemistry, neuroanatomy, quantum collapses, future outcomes of decisions, etc., it is all determined without your participation or input. That is what "Determinism" means.

Gary:

i have been asked for a more concise version of this explanation as it is a question that is frequently asked.

To believe that we had conscious "free will" and control at a quantum level, we would have to be continuously aware, every microsecond, of every atom in our finger nail and be deciding exactly what it would do. At the same time, we would have to be making the same decisions for every atom in our left ear, right knee, and tip of our nose, etc. Then the next microsecond, do it again, and again, and again...it's just not possible.

nonexistent:

Hi Gary,

Totally agree.

I would like to add, quantum theory argument is often brought up in support of existence of free will. I understand how it might counter the idea of strict determinism of the Existence, but it can't prove free will. Even if macro-level events, like human thought and behaviors could be affected by sub atomic quantum states (which is very questionable), then it would just mean that these events are affected or caused by quantum states. So there is still no place for free will here, just broader causation of the events.

Unknown:

Great post. I really like the closing, which is not triumphant or full of conviction, but is instead a recognition that argument won't resolve this, only inquiry. The key to it really is the deconstruction of the "I". Then the science makes one slap the forehead in obvious validation. With the science, maybe peeps will be encouraged to do the inquiry, whether they can help it or not :)

Gary:

Hi Unknown,

Yes, that is the critical "point". If you are "predetermined" to be drawn to self-inquiry, and to practice diligently, and let go of your attachments, stories, and fears, you need to get on with it.

Saif:

So if there's no free will then I have no obligation to try and improve my self and my life?

Gary:

Hi Saif,

That's correct, since you have no free will or control, nor does anyone else, you have no obligation to "try and improve my self and my life", simply because there is no one, no Saif, no others, to have it.

If you do the self-inquiry, you will find as i did that there is no "I" there, which the neuroscience confirms, which makes the entire debate meaningless and the understanding obvious.

That doesn't mean that your life may not improve, or go exactly the opposite of the way "you" wanted it to go, as it will be totally out of your control. The big surprise for "me" was that "my life" was running so much better without "me" in it, particularly as nothing that i wanted to have happen, happened.

What did happen, serendipitously and out of my control, was so much more wonderful and exciting than what "i" had planned, that it was easy to just let go and completely surrender to whatever manifested. It was clear that whatever was running "my life" was much better at it than i was and had connections, knowledge and powers far beyond mine.

Guillaume Tremblay:

Nice review of free will Gary.

It's become clear to me that the neuroscience clearly demonstrating there's no free will shatters the paradigm of a "me", which essentially is why it is so disconcerting to many. The science thrusts us, willingly or not, into the reality that there is just nature in action, no "me". I am moved and determined by the forces of nature just as much as the hornet, the deer or the tree.

I love Sam Harris' example of Katrina vs 911, how nature could resolve its problems so much more effectively under this new paradigm.

Gary:

Hi Guillaume,

Yes, as the "I/me/my" is the core of "free will", its unveiling as just a phantom created by a piece of software which needs updating, is a major shift in one's fundamental understanding. In a discussion on FB yesterday, this arose from "nowhere":

"There is an "I" program running, along with a lot of other programs, and the "I" program believes it is in control of the other programs and can tell them what to do. However, it turns out that the System Administrator just put that "i'm in charge" code in the "I" program so it stayed interested in what was happening, not to give it control. The other programs continue to do what they have always been doing and run paying little/no attention to the "I" program as its output has a very low signal/noise ratio, it is always after the fact, and nothing it says ever comes out the way it says it will."

you also touch on a very important aspect of "no free will" which Sam Harris did a nice job on, that we will treat others better when we understand that they don't have any free will either.

Patrick:

Hi Gary,

thank you again for knocking the bottom out of my bucket last year. Permit me to add another heading to your list of philosophical postures on free will:

Affirm it

See the preface to Part V of Spinoza's Ethics, "Of the Power of the Understanding, or of Human Freedom"

"Lastly, I omit all the assertions which he (Descartes) makes concerning the will and its freedom, inasmuch as I have abundantly proved that his premises are false. "

Gary:

Hi Patrick,

Great that your bucket has no bottom. That is one of the great Zen metaphors, even used by Bassui in his self-inquiry classic from 14th century Japan, "Dharma Talk On One Mind", (1) a very important text in my journey:

"Your long-held conceptions and notions will perish, after absolute questioning, in the way that every drop of water vanishes from a tub broken open at the bottom, and perfect enlightenment will follow like flowers suddenly blooming on withered trees."

Hadn't seen the Spinoza discourse, but it is a powerful one. Spinoza was, as you no doubt know, "Einstein's philosopher", and there is little in his work that isn't perhaps the best that philosophy has to offer. Thanks for the share.

Beau Taillefer:

Thanks for this article Gary.

Sam Harris seems to be the most logical and useful in this area compared to the other philosophers. It's interesting that he's also well researched and educated about there not being a "self", something many philosophers don't want to touch.

I've seen some people react negatively when given demonstrations/arguments that there is no free will. The "negative" reaction, whether it's in mood or behavior, is coming from an individual that still has a selfing network running and is now responding to these new ideas as threats. It's amazing to watch people armor themselves against an idea.

I've always been extremely skeptical of pseudo claims that quantum mechanics is somehow giving individuals free will, and I'm glad you're addressing that in these comments.

Keep the blogs posts coming Gary, I'm making my way through all of your old posts and it's getting hard to think of a new question that hasn't been asked!

-from Her to Her

Gary:

Hi Beau.

Great that you found it so useful. As you point out, it is a very emotional issue with many folk, as i've seen over the years of talking about it. Nothing sparks so much anger, fear, and hostility as challenging the belief in "free will". After one talk @ SAND in San Rafael four or five years ago, i was told that "someone is going to kill you".

Yes, it was good that the quantum mechanics question got asked, as that is a big misconception, not for the scientists, but for those who know some of the science but haven't had a chance to work through it in detail.

A great comment that you can't find "a new question that hasn't been asked". If you do find an area that you feel needs some coverage, don't hesitate to contact me.

stillness, from Her to Her

Also agree on Sam Harris, who is a real anomaly as he has both a Ph.D. from UCLA in cognitive neuroscience and strong philosophy background with a B.A. from Stanford. he also spent a lot of time in India studying meditation with Buddhist and Hindu masters and was raised a Quaker with a secular background. i don't agree w/everything he says, but he is the best of the bunch. (2)

Unknown:

Great Article Gary. If we do live in a pre-determined universe / world, what is the point of our pre-determined existence? Is it to just experience and observe? Is our pre-determined life trajectory a product of Karma? Do we have no free -will even in choosing our attitude in any circumstances? Or is our attitude also predetermined, even if we do appear to choose our attitude (stoicism)?

If we free ourselves of our behavioral conditioning are things still predetermined? If our 'I' is destroyed through awakening, is there a greater will (divine Will)? Is this will also predetermined, or is their free will, when the little I is freed of the limited confines of the conditioned self? Lots of questions here :-)

Thanks Gary.

Gary:

Hi Unknown.

my ongoing experience, given all of the many serendipities of infinitesimal probability and great value that manifest every day, and the precognitions that occur, it is clear that "something" is running things that is far more intelligent, omnipresent, and interconnected than i am. i have found that "my life" runs better w/o "me" in it.

Given our current cosmological research, we know that there is an all pervasive field, called the Higgs field which can manifest matter as described in the blogpost "How 'consciousness' creates matter...the God particle". (3)

As it is clear that everything in this Field (which is everything) is evolving, it follows that whatever is running things is also evolving, so it then follows that "we" are evolutionary-sensing-experiencing manifestations of the field to allow it to evolve through these "bodies", and all forms and objects.

i have no sense of having any "free will" at any level, simply because there is no one to have it.

Sean M:

One concern is that, though the research and the experience of a few shows the impossibility of free will, the vast majority of human beings still believe in free will. I think one of the traps of "neo-Advaita" is the premature leap to claiming "there is no free will"/"there is no doer" without concretely embodying this fact. The mouth proclaims that there is no self while the mind is the host of a parasitic ego. I wonder what to make of the Intelligence that seems to reinforce the idea of multiple, discrete operators.

Gary:

Hi Sean M.,

Good comments.

As the recent video "Are 'we' just outdated, buggy programs?" discusses, the "I" is just a program that (Cosmic) Intelligence inserted into our OS about 75,000 years ago. (4)

At the time, as our species was growing in number and we needed to coordinate more complex activities with different assignments, we needed to assign different tasks to different folk, so we created a symbolic, subject/doing/object language. With that capability, we swept our four other humanoid competitors away, and we were able to dominate the planet, for "good" or "ill".

None of this really "needed" the subroutine of "free will", but it apparently seemed like "a good idea at the time" to install some feeling/sense of "ownership" to drive the overall effort forward. Those of our species who didn't have it so strongly didn't do as well as those who did.

Now it is apparent that the "I" program, and its subroutine of "free will" are desperately in need of a major upgrade. With the increasing evidence of there being no "free will", which the Intelligence is causing to manifest, along with the understanding around the "I" itself being a big problem, this is happening. This is, on an evolutionary time scale, occurring very rapidly, so it seems like Intelligence is doing an "uninstall", albeit like MSFT, not well written or timely.

Anonymous:

Gary, does this debate have anything to do with nature/nurture or is the point that there just isn't any free will whether we're influenced by either nature or nurture?

Gary:

Hi Anonymous,

Yes, that is the point, "there just isn't any free will", whether we like it or not and whether it is both nature and nurture, or mostly one or the other, we're not in control of what is going on and we have no real choices.

So just let go of that outdated belief and enjoy the dance that "something else", with powers, intelligence and knowledge far beyond ours is performing for Her evolution.

ARE OUR LIVES CONTROLLED BY OUR UNCONSCIOUS BRAIN?

Guillaume Tremblay

It's really such an interesting paradox that seems to just have to be accepted. It's as though only stillness can understand "no free will" and the narrative mind simply cannot grasp this concept.

I read the Gita, your blogs and e-mail, the words of Ramana, which all say persevere, persevere, persevere, which feels true. And yet the mind seems bewildered, who's persevering?

With no free will, who's choosing to persevere? Is it the Self telling itself to persevere? The narrative mind seems to run in circles trying to answer this. "I don't know" followed by a quiet mind seems to be the answer that feels the best. A wonderful mystery.

Gary:

Hi Guillaume.

Hi Guillaume. Yes, the "narrative mind", which relies very heavily on the existence of the I/me/my, "free will", "choice" and "being in control" for its reason for being and mode of operation is deeply troubled, confused and afraid of that all vanishing and then "runs in circles". It raises these questions like "With no free will, who's choosing to persevere?", etc. to attempt to derail the process.

The question to then ask is "Who's asking that question?" and "What is it that is afraid of these questions?". your "I don't know' followed by a quiet mind" is also a great response and you can tell that by what you indicated - it "feels the best". As discussed in the blogpost "Feeling your way to nondual awakening", always feel your way to what works best for you. That is the most reliable guide i have found in this work. (1)

And, as you mentioned, persevere, persevere, persevere.

OUR "CHOICES" ARE RANDOM?...NEW RESEARCH

Erik King:

Gary,

If it is true that we have no freewill, has our will been reduced to deterministic behavior based on external stimuli and internal biological needs? And if so, do you believe we are simply products of a simulation being executed or are all probabilities being played out (everything is happening everywhere) and we are merely collapsing our perceived reality through our collective observations?

I would be interested in getting your thoughts on this subject.

Thanks,

Gary:

Hi Eric,

In my experience, when the "page turned", it was clear that as "I" did not exist, that there was no one to be in control, so there was no free will. However, as what happened to "my life" occurred, it was clear even with no one "in control", that my life was massively serendipitous and was clearly not random, i.e. there was "order" to it. These serendipitous events involved many individual events that had infinitesimal probabilities, and had to have occurred in a specific sequence at precisely the right time. They also appeared to be "positive" for my spiritual unfoldment, although they weren't necessarily "pleasant".

There was also an astonishingly powerful "something" behind all of this that felt supportive...the more that i surrendered, the more that "something" somehow "held" and supported me. As i surrendered fully, i felt totally held and supported.

It was obvious that "I" had no ability to arrange such things as i didn't know anything about the folk or countless events that had preceded these events in such a perfect arrangement and sequence, so one possibility was that they were perfectly predetermined far in the distant past. Their unfolding was determined by Darwinian principles, adapting to the environments and conditions as they unfolded, to incrementally increase the probability that those genes would be propagated.

If you read "The Moral Animal" by my good friend at Princeton, the evolutionary psychologist Robert Wright, there is very little that is not underlain by Darwinian principles including much adaptation to changing environments. (1)

The other alternative is that there is a massive field of great intelligence that we are all part of, and It/She is using us as evolutionary, explorer pods to evolve Herself and She operates w/capabilities far beyond our understanding. In this dynamic situation, there would be constant maximization as things evolved, on a picosecond by picosecond basis.

Another alternative is that both are occurring. Darwinian evolution holds as a template, but "something" is changing the environments to direct elements of the process. my experience of this "something" is so strong that it can't be purely "mechanistic".

There is a video "Predestination, control, free will and the illusion of time" that you might find interesting as well. (2)

THE IMPOSSIBILITY OF "FREE WILL"... SCIENTIFICALLY AND LOGICALLY

Roy Dopson

Freedom from the burden of choice is liberation.

G

Hi Roy.

Totally agree.

It is amazing how directly freedom from the illusion/burden of believing you have free will and are in control liberates one from the egoic/doer structure. With it goes the illusion of good deeds and bad deeds.

Instead of "life" continuing to be a terrifying place believing one is in control, one discovers that life with the understanding that free will is a delusion, is easy, sweet and liberated and so much "safer" than before.

Vallor

Sir,

You seem to have argued that your meditations have destroyed your capability for free will. I think that is mistaken -- but simply put, it's not (yet?) possible to dispute the self-reporting of mental states. So, three possibilities exist: a) The "free will is an illusion" people are mistaken, b) The "free will is not an illusion" people are mistaken, or c) Some human minds have free will, and some don't.

if (c) is correct, how should those of us with free will treat these unfortunately brothers and sisters, who are unable to make decisions for themselves?

And if you perceive that this is a koan -- good insight. ;P

G

Hi Vallor.

That's not what i've "argued". As i said in the post, with the deconstruction of the "I", it was obvious that i never had free will as there was no one to have it, nor was there free will before - i just believed there was.

The big surprise, and i had been a fervent believer in free will, was that my life went on as before, even better, w/o the belief that i had a free will and had any control over what happened immediately or its ultimate result.

Your c) is a logical impossibility. How in our massively-interconnected network of today's global society could there be some population that had free will and others that didn't? Just how would that operate?

Everyone would have to wait around for those w/free will to make a decision before they knew what to do. As the smallest decision in south India could ultimately impact some seemingly unrelated activity in France or Brazil (Complex Systems Theory), how would that work?

It isn't a question of only certain folk being "unable to make decisions for themselves". The neuroscience demonstrates that none of us can make meaningful decisions on the outcomes of our actions.

Another way to look at it, using Complex Systems understanding, is that we have no idea what the outcome is of any of our actions as the results of those actions work their forward through time impacting countless unknown others in unknown ways.

Even if we had "free will", which our science has demonstrated we don't, we have no way to know or even project what the outcomes of our actions will be. How can we believe we have meaningful "control"? And over what?

Nate Blair

This was solved definitively for hundreds of years by every middle school youth who bothered to think carefully.

G

Hi Nate.

Absolutely agree. i was amazed, once i started to look carefully, and as i have worked w/others, how obvious it is. Where do our thoughts come from? Do i think up my thoughts, or what i say, "ahead of time"?

Or as i frequently ask others, if you believe you have free will and are "in control", how's that working out for you? If it isn't working out, why do you still believe that it's true?

i believe most folk know, really know, at some level, that it's not working and they have no free will or control, but are just terrified to face the possibility and admit it. That's why there is such forceful "push back".

If "free will" was obviously true, and certain, and really worked, folk would just laugh the whole thing off. They don't. It makes them angry. Why is that?

Anonymous

Dear Dr. Weber,

I would like to express my sincere thanks to you for providing such a spiritually insightful blog and your youtube lectures are simply outstanding!

I have personally experienced (since at least intellectually realizing that all events are predetermined and working to consciously integrate predeterminism into my moment to moment stream of thoughts) that I have become very complacent in my everyday life.

Upon realizing that every action I take has enormous and unpredictable repercussions, I have become more risk-averse. I have been spending a greater amount time staying at the house. I have become less communicative with my partner, family and friends, out of fear that I will not be able to predict and determine what I will say, and my autonomic and spontaneous utterances may inadvertently hurt those I love.

Of course, I am determined to behave this way as the result of prior mental and environmental states. I cannot predict and control what I will think, say or do for the remainder of my existence. I am just a biological automaton who will exhibit automatic responses to internal and external inputs.

This knowledge has created a sense of helplessness and fear, that though I may personally not be responsible for what I do, the world will still hold me accountable for what I do, and that I may be reproached and penalized for the mistakes and blunders I may make in the future.

Please pardon me if I have wasted your time and I welcome any insights you could provide to help me.

G

Hi Anonymous.

Realize that this new understanding that you have no free will, and no ability to predict all of the results of your actions on countless others, is not a new situation...it has always been that way, only now you have a correct understanding of it.

These actions that have manifested of (perceived) changes in your actions and communication w/others are also not in your control; they will either stay that way or they will change to some other actions.

The most important thing to remember is that there are stories behind these changes, and they are generated by the I/ego that was at the root of the illusion of "free will" or "control". If you just ask simply, "Are these stories true?", "How do i feel when i have these stories in consciousness?", "Could i let go of these stories?", "Are these stories helpful?". The blogpost "Surrendering the 'I', letting go of suffering" has more details. (1)

The ego/I phantom/avatar will create all sorts of stories, doubts, concerns, and problems w/this new understanding of "no free will". Its very survival is dependent on maintaining this illusion. Inquire into "Who/what it is that has these concerns?", "What is afraid of hurting (or helping) others?", "Where is this one that believed it was in control before, but was clearly wrong about that?".

you will find, as Ramana Maharshi has said, "What is destined to happen will happen. If you are destined not to work, work cannot be had even if you hunt for it. If you are destined to work, you will not be able to avoid it and you will be forced to engage yourself in it. So, leave it to the higher power; you cannot renounce or retain as you choose." (2)

The same applies to your communication w/others, or your perceived decision to be or to not be active, you cannot renounce or retain as you choose.

Anonymous

I was predestined to leave this comment.

G

Yes, indeed you were and the fascinating part of it is that you have no idea what the outcome of this seemingly simple action will be and who will be impacted by it as it works its way forward through "time" and "space".

Someone reading your comment will have their life changed by the few seconds they take to read it, even if they reject the premise entirely. They may find it is the critical element that they have been waiting for and it may change their life entirely, or not. What they say to others may change them, positively, negatively or not, etc.

That is why it is so obviously out of our control and ability to predict.

Anonymous

I find this topic fascinating! Could you tell me how this research would apply to long-term planning?

Such as, I just got back from a vacation. We planned everything out, fleshed out the schedule, and made hotel reservations. We then went on the trip (and had a great time!). It seems as if we made the plans well in advance and then were determined to carry them out. I know that in the moment, we could have spontaneously decided not to board the plane or not to go to a certain museum, but what about the overall vacation that we went on?

Also, what about buying a house or planning a new business venture or even planning something like a wedding?

How does planning come into play?

Thank you for your time

G

Hi Anonymous. you will continue to do "long-term planning"...How else can you make plane or hotel reservations and schedule all of the events you want to attend? you can't just show up at the airport, or hotel and be certain that you can get a flight/room, etc. you can even make up "to do" lists for every day, and plan new business initiatives, or even start-ups.

However, realize that none of it may take place, or a totally different agenda may manifest, and that all of this is out of your control. If you had gotten to the airport, and a "mechanical problem" or "weather" several states away has delayed your plane, then your entire vacation is changed, "out of your control".

i spent years working w/folk in start-ups and i never saw an original business plan that didn't change; everyone, including the investors, knew it would change, but it was a place to start. It was acknowledged by all concerned that it was "out of their control". Markets change, customers change, competitors change, the over-all investment and economy changes, technology changes, etc. so the plan is changed completely "out of your control".

i can recall in one meeting chiding our CEO (gently), on our using the economic forecast to feed into our business planning, since it was always wrong, always. He said "Well, we have to use something, even if it's always wrong."

Planning is useful...it's just important to recognize up front that that isn't what's going to manifest, that it's not your fault, and you need to be flexible at adapting to the reality.

Anonymous

Thank you so much for the response. It really helps to clear things up. After reading your response, I started thinking about how much I relate to this since I am an artist. Generally, the idea I have at the beginning of a project is very different then the end result. Neither outcome is better or worse, just different. While I am making creative decisions in the moment, it is some-what automatic. If I relate this to the way a person lives his/her life, then it makes a lot of sense. Thank you for the insight!

G

Great that you found it useful. As you may have heard, i "backed into" the "no free will" understanding. i was very deterministic until my self-referential thoughts stopped, and the "I" fell away. Then it was obvious there was no one to be in control, or to have "free will", nor had there ever been.

Instead of being a dreaded, chaotic, troubled, space, i found that understanding to be one of the most freeing, enabling, and beautiful things that ever happened. All of my "sins", "regrets", "failures", etc. fell away, as did my "achievements", "accomplishments", etc. (which were even more disempowering that my failures) and i was just left in "now, now, now", fully present for whatever arose.

It is such a magnificent way to live.

Jose Antonio

Hello Gary.

Thanks for this blog and your two books, they are helping me a lot with my daily practice and to understand many things.

After reading a few times many of your posts, I don't fully understand one thing, and I think I'm missing something. Regarding "free will", I understand that the "I/ego" doesn't do anything (no choices), that She/Universal Consciousness does it. Ramana says that everything is predetermined, even smaller things; so when a person is going to be born and die, which experiences he going to have and what people he is going to meet are already predetermined, and that our only choice is whether to identify with the screen or the movie (but even that is not our choice).

My multiple-question is: can the I/ego do something, are these self-referential thoughts or DMN/blah - blah network as well predetermined, or can we choose to work in stopping these self-referential thoughts? When I'm working with self-inquiry to stop these self-referential thoughts (I/ego), who is doing it, She/Universal Consciousness or the ego?

I used to think that this I/ego (blah-blah network) is the only thing that has some kind of "free will" (just to think, not to do), and depending of your progress in surrender this I/ego, She/Universal Consciousness will arrange things to show you "the way". But I'm not sure anymore.

G

Hi Jose,

Predetermination doesn't mean, in my experience, that the Universal Consciousness put something in place long ago that is working its way forward, like a giant clock to carry out events.

What is more likely, is that since everything is changing and evolving constantly, that the Universal Consciousness is also evolving and learning constantly through us, as She also has to evolve to survive. There is much good research now on galaxies disappearing into black holes and other new ones being created out of the "bottoms" of black holes.

As this process goes on moment-to-moment, whatever the ego/I is doing is part of that, at least as long as it exists. If the ego/I continues to identify with the movie/ screen, which is out of its control, it will remain and suffering will continue as part of the Universal Consciousness' evolutionary, learning process.

Whether or not, when, and if the energy/motivation arises to deconstruct the ego/I is not under its own control. It can't be because if the ego/I had "free will", it would never decide to deconstruct itself, as it likes the current arrangement just fine.

Arthur

Dear Gary

Thanks for your very lucid article, I enjoyed reading it and Sam's book on Free Will. While I can't fault any of the logic presented I do think there are unanswered questions, ultimately connecting to the "hard problem" of consciousness. Hopefully you'll see what I mean…

Basically, if all this is an illusion, then we have to explain WHY we have this illusion in the first place. There are a few surface level explanations that spring to mind.

1) We predict others actions based on the past and the future. When we base explanations on the future we assume people have goals/purpose. Behaviors deliberately directed toward goals have the feeling of being free or choice driven. "I want a new car so I'm going to choose to do xyz". When we based explanations on the past or conditions then they don't have that flavor…In most every day social situations the explanation involving the goal-directed behavior is more efficient and less clunky. Predicting others accurately and efficiently obviously has fitness advantages. We then apply that same process of explanation to our own actions.

2) Even if our narrative explanations are post-hoc, you could argue they influence future behavior by cycling back into unconscious conditions for the next time. E.g. If I smoke a cigarette, then consciously really regret the "choice", that regret might alter my neurology such that I don't smoke next time. I may never have had a real choice about whether to smoke or not, but the belief that I did made me feel a certain way that did influence future behavior. There's still no free will, but the post-hoc narrative is doing something.

3) Blame and praise. The things we think we have a choice about are behaviors responsive to blame and praise. There's no point blaming my gut for rumbling because doing so won't change the noises it makes. But blame and shame me for e.g. undressing in public, and I'll be much less likely to do this again. Again, none of it is free, but it helps explain why the illusion might be there – the illusion is basically an evolutionary short hand that confers fitness via our ability to change behavior by how we interact with others and ourselves...

G

Hi Arthur,

... IMHO, a key reason free will "seemed like a good idea at the time" was that it gave us the illusion that we, and others, were in control so we would develop guilt for "bad behaviors" that didn't support the integrity of the hierarchy and got us tossed out of the cave.

It really didn't change our behaviors, as anyone who has fully understood that it is an illusion will tell you, as you behave as you have always behaved, only w/o the guilt and w/o the blaming of others.

i haven't seen that the "free will" program has any positive effect on stopping any addictive habits, like smoking, porn, alcohol, social media, gambling, etc. If it did, we wouldn't have any problem dropping them. If anything, it only creates guilt that we haven't been able to stop, which feeds the monster.

An interesting discussion, but the most important thing is to recognize that realizing that we don't have control, or free will, or anyone to have them, is just how much easier, and more "full of wonder" your life becomes.

I GET "NO FREE WILL" INTELLECTUALLY, BUT CAN'T MAKE IT "REAL"...WHAT TO DO?

SK,

Dear Gary,

Recently, by both scriptural study and introspection, I am beginning to settle on the realization that free will is an illusion. Our thoughts and actions, even this very email, are automated processes without any volition. The only thing that seems to be distinct from these is my own consciousness ("I am" and "I exist"). These rise from within me and manifest without my volition.

I had the good fortune of coming across your blog. The biggest question is, **isn't this very process of finding enlightenment a predetermined process?** Can **I** achieve enlightenment or is it more accurate to say that enlightenment happens to me? The idea that the very process of finding enlightenment is subject to the mandates of fate is very disconcerting. Hoping you could shed some light on the above question.

G. Hi SK,

you have seen the blogpost "You say 'we have no free will', and "we're not in control"...Is that experience, science or philosophy?" There is very little doubt w/in most of the cognitive neuroscience community that free will is an evolutionarily-derived construct, something that our brains manifested evolutionarily. (1)

i spoke @ the TSC conference in Stockholm and there wasn't even a serious doubt about there not being free will. The main point was whether folk should be told the "truth", or not. i've worked a lot w/the Yale cognitive neuroscience folk and gave a talk to a Yale meditation group and free will came up. i mentioned the Stockholm conference and a Yale faculty member who was there said he was at the conference and agreed.

Logically, and necessarily, it follows that even "enlightenment" is predetermined. The blogs and the video "Everything is Predetermined; Einstein and Ramana Maharshi on Free Will" showed that Ramana Maharshi was very clear that everything is predetermined, even the smallest things. (2)

On a few occasions Ramana did tell some folk that our only choice was whether to identify with the screen or the movie, but, IMHO even that is not our choice. Whether we will be able to make that distinction is out of our control. Ramana adapted answers to each questioner; i believe this was an example.

That is also my lived experience. i was a highly determined Ph.D. with a lot of success and was certain that i had "done it all myself".

When my self-referential thoughts abruptly stopped, i had 1000 folk working for me, four research labs and a budget of $260MM. i found that everything went along perfectly w/no self-referential thoughts, no apparent "doer" of anything, or anyone who could manifest "free will". There was no logical alternative.

The same is true for "my" awakening" process. There were many serendipitous twists and turns, spiritual teachers of many types, many insights, different practices, etc. The big shift occurred unexpectedly, not where, when, or how it was expected. What manifested was beyond anything i could have imagined.

SK

Hi Gary,

I really appreciate that you took the time to respond. Am struggling recently with these questions and it's very reassuring to find someone who can understand. A few of my family and friends understand where I am coming from. It reveals the hold that the illusion of free will has on humanity. Some questions:

1. The debate regarding whether folks should be "told the truth". Did a realization of your lack of volition lead to a more fulfilling/enriching (i.e. happy life)? A friend attests that although he knows free will is an illusion, he chooses to live in it and finds beauty in the very illusion itself. Is that a misguided belief?

2. Why do I have a visceral aversion to the lack of free will? How did the illusion even develop? If we operate in a deterministic framework, how can we comprehend free will? Isn't that analogous to a blind man believing that he has an understanding of color?

3. Enlightenment, in Eastern thought is the realization of an Ultimate Truth. Is the realization that we do not possess free will analogous to the realization/enlightenment of Hinduism/Buddhism/Vedanta? What are similarities and differences? How does the realization fit into the broader frameworks/goals of Eastern thought?

4. What would you recommend for me to do at this stage? I'm beginning to develop an intellectual understanding of fate/free will/determinism but I don't feel any more "peaceful". Any tips/recommendations?

...as Einstein said, a comprehension that you're not in control does make you take yourself a little less seriously.

G.

Re 1., the big surprise was that realizing there was "no free will" was unlike what was expected which was living in terror and fear. Life is/was blissful, easy. It's a dance rather than a war. i recognized that i wasn't responsible for the world, but that it was doing fine just by "itself" w/o my involvement.

At some level we all know that is the truth - that we aren't in control. we keep failing at "making things happen" as we wanted, and keep feeling insecure and frightened. Once it is realized, you're "off the hook" and relax into the reality you've been arguing with unsuccessfully for so long.

Re 2, we developed this aversion to a lack of free will as we like to believe that we can control things and if we give up our illusion, we will be at the mercy of things which we can't control; we're just afraid.

As to why "free will" developed, it's not clear how it is functionally, evolutionarily adaptive. Perhaps when the world was much, much simpler it seemed like it worked.

Re 3, awakening happened for "me" before, but just before, it became obvious that there was no free will as there was no one to have it. They were roughly simultaneous; once the "I" is seen through, it all just collapses.

As to how it all fits into "Eastern thought", that is a broad topic as it is hardly homogeneous. There is supposedly no word in Sanskrit, the root-tongue of the romance languages, for "free will".

Re 4 on some helpful "questions" to aid in your understanding of the lack of free will and control, ask yourself, when an event happens:

Could i have reasonably expected this to happen as it did?

Was it probabilistically likely?

What else had to happen to everyone involved to make this come about just as it did?

Can i predict all outcomes of this event on everyone involved and everyone they come in contact with in the future?

Did i consciously choose for this to occur as it did?

Keep these questions active. They will be helpful for disabusing yourself of the illusion. If you see enough examples in "real life", the brain will let go.

SK. Thank you so much! The responses definitely helped.

Re Point #3, from my understanding, the "awakening", or "realization" depicted by mystics such as Ramana Maharishi, Meister Eckhart, and Eckhart Tolle is a state of unity in which we understand that we are a part of a Universal Consciousness, and there is a termination of the "I-thought" or ego.

I do believe with increasing certainty that we are without control. This is increasingly accepted by my mind. **Is this realization the same as the realization that there is no "I"?** Or is the "lack of volition" realization a subset of the greater awakening? Or is the "lack of volition" understanding completely independent of the greater awakening?

I have faith that my mind can accept my lack of volition as a perfectly reasonable way to exist in the world. I will keep inquiring to coax my brain into accepting the paradigm.

G. A few folk i work w/, get "no free will/no control" almost immediately. Subsequently, they had to be reminded, which was no problem. Some folk still have some work to do for full "awakening", despite significant progress.

Others progressed a great ways w/o even discussing "no free will"; it later became obvious.

IME, if one awakens fully into "no self", it is impossible to assert that "I am in control", and "I have free will", because there is no one to have it or do it. The illusion of "free will" just falls away.

i am introducing it earlier in my work w/folk. It is very useful for deconstructing the "I". Even if folk reject it, it is possible to get most folk to "maybe that's true, at least sometimes". However, even if it is totally rejected, this does weaken its hold, as at some level, it has been considered as being possible. This begins to weaken the associated neural networks.

The "I" already knows that it is not in control. It has been struggling mightily to make everything work out as planned, despite countless failures (and successes) that it had no part in, which it recognizes. The brain ultimately welcomes the new paradigm and life flows freely and easily when the situation is recognized clearly and fully. Being in control was a hopeless task all along.

You say "we have no free will" and "we're not in control"...Is that experience, science, or philosophy?

Q.

You say that "we have no free will", and "we're not in control". That has been debated forever by philosophers and religions. Everyone knows that they have free will and that they make many choices in everyday life. Why do you say we don't have free will?

G.

That is an important question in this work. It deeply impacts how we feel about past choices and actions, as well as how much stress and anxiety arise as we plan for the future.

... for some "enlightening" scientific insights, let's look at complexity and chaos theory and how it applies to free will and control. Complex systems theory deals with interactions between parts of a system and how they affect the behavior of the entire system and how it interacts with its environment.

A complex system occurs when interconnected parts have behaviors that affect the whole system in ways that are not obvious from the properties of the individual parts. A system with many parts displays "disorganized complexity".

This approach has been used to understand ant colonies, economies, financial systems, social structures, climate, nervous systems, cells, energy and telecommunication infrastructures, etc. Most systems of interest to us are complex systems.

...the fundamental equation of complex systems does yield the famous "Butterfly Effect", which is the metaphor of a hurricane in the Atlantic Ocean being caused by a butterfly flapping its wings in France (or wherever)...

Applied to free will and "control", several useful principles arise from complex systems:

> *a) All parts of the system affect, and are affected by, many other parts of the system in a complex web of cause and effect and feedback.*

> *b) Completely unpredictable results can emerge even if the original conditions are known in great detail.*

> *c) Complex interacting systems undergoing change (our lives) are unpredictable.*

> *d) With all the interactions and feedback, staggeringly vast amounts of information are required for even a simple decision. A decision a second later would need completely new information as everything had changed. (1)*

we have no idea what our actions will produce over time, who they will affect, and in what way. we also have no idea how our current situation came to be as it is, or whose actions will affect us.

Useful science also comes from work in cognitive neuroscience on free will which began w/Benjamin Libet's work, discussed in the blogs "Free will vs neuroscience; belief vs science" and "no sin, no karma, no good deeds, no bad deeds". Libet's experiments showed clearly that the motor cortex initiates an action well before the "I" is even told about it, and in advance of the action being performed. If we aren't even aware when, or what, action is initiated, how can we be "in control" and where is our "free will"? (2)

Libet's work, which received the inaugural "Virtual Nobel Prize in Psychology", not surprisingly caused a firestorm of reactions, and great hostility from many sides, including other scientists. Nonetheless, in the intervening 40 years, w/much more sophisticated technology and measuring equipment and many studies by many folk, his work stands.

A third scientific approach comes from genetics. The Nobel Prize Winner Francis Crick, the molecular biologist and neuroscientist who, with James D. Watson, discovered the structure of DNA, stated that:

> *"You, your joys and your sorrows, your memories and your ambitions, your sense of personal identity and your free will, are in fact no more than the behavior of a vast assembly of nerve cells and their associated molecules." (3)*

...That genetics, depending on how it is defined, is a major element defining "us" is widely-accepted. The question is how much "we" are defined by genetics and epigenetics, or "nature", and how much "we" are defined by family, friends, where and when we were born, what our environment and experiences were, etc. or "nurture".

Since none of this is w/in our control, there is still no free will, but the mix of "nature" and "nurture" is complex, interrelated and likely inseparable.

FREE WILL VERSUS NEUROSCIENCE: BELIEF VS SCIENCE

Q.

I believe that I have clear choices because that has been the basis of my spiritual guidance for twenty years. The existence of neural correlates to any given behavior or cognitive process is merely that: a correlate...there are neural correlates to what is happening, and...physiological processes which you not directly control...much that we do not have control over, but this is not evidence of...absence of choice...

One of the big problems with all this science...is that our cognitive science is still primitive...

Once recent paper...in biology reviewed the most cited literature...couple of decades ago - over a ten year period or so. About 40% of the findings... subsequently...highly flawed or dead wrong. I wonder how flawed will these neuro-imaging papers be in a couple of decades...

G. There is no question that what science has proven and is investigating in any field, including cognitive neuroscience, constantly changes. That is how empirical investigation works, in science and also in our spiritual practices. Consistency is only possible if one operates totally on belief...

As an example of the changing nature of scientific experimentation, let's take telescopes...often regarded as the beginning of modern science.

Galileo...the "Father of Modern Science", built a telescope and found the four moons of Jupiter, the phases of Venus, and sunspots. He also found that the earth was not the center of our universe, and that, in fact, the sun was and the earth and the other planets rotated around it.

Prior to this, descriptions of what we saw in the heavens were based only on what everyone could see with their own eyes. Everyone believed that was the true picture, so much so that it was the basis for religious dogma.

...As Galileo's work directly contradicted a fundamental belief of the church, he was investigated by the Inquisition in 1615, which ruled that this was only a possibility, not a fact. Galileo then wrote...the first real scientific paper documenting his discoveries. The Inquisition...then retried Galileo and his work and found it "vehemently suspect of heresy"...and put him under house arrest for the rest of his life.

Since 1608, more powerful...telescopes emerged to detect x-rays, ultraviolet, infrared, far-infrared radiations, etc., from land and in space....black holes, anti-matter, countless galaxies and universes, etc. were found...To your way of thinking, science has been wrong, continuously for 400 years...

Not until 1822 did the church lift the ban on Galileo's work, but they would not pardon him. Finally, in 1992, three years after the "Galileo" spacecraft probe and orbiter had been launched to Jupiter, the Vatican...officially conceded that "the earth was not stationary". (However, there was still controversy in 2008, which has not been resolved, on whether the earth was the center of the galaxy.) (1)

That is the difference between science and belief.

As with telescope development, the huge increase in neuroscientific efforts, technologies and devices has consistently demonstrated that Libet's original finding that the "I" does not initiate actions, the brain does, was correct.

Epilogue

Self-inquiry, letting go of our attachments and recognizing that we are not these thoughts, mind or bodies, can update the brain's operating system to meet contemporary demands. It is challenging because it is so simple and direct. Societal and institutional resistance is strong. Perseverance in practices is essential as the brain takes time and data to modify evolutionarily-installed programs.

If our species doesn't change its software, it will not go well for us.

She does everything.

ACKNOWLEDGEMENTS

Unless you've skipped ahead, you know by now that Universal Consciousness/ She does everything…everything, even the smallest things, including writing this book.

No book manifests without much support from individual perturbations in the Field of Universal Consciousness masquerading for Her dance.

In addition to those folk already mentioned in the book, Rich Doyle, Suzanne Winters, Christina Guimond, Kevin Hackett and Adam Engle provided valuable insights and perspectives.

Many gasshos to Oskar K. Linares for our dialogues and for the sumi-e paintings in the book.

Ramana Maharshi's work was seminal. Gratitude to the folk at Ramanasramam who published the most useful and comprehensive version of the Ribhu Gita in Sanskrit, along with many books on his teachings, and the dedication picture.

Gratitude for the hundreds of folk with whom i have had the privilege of working 1/1 - an enormous source of insights and probing questions.

Additional information is available at www.happiness-beyond-thought. com including a listing of books, presentations, articles, interviews, blog, MP3 links, youTube channel, soundcloud channel and a comprehensive bio.

References

INTRODUCTION

1. Josephenson, T., www.brainyquote.com/quotes/quotes/t/terryjosep107153. html, extracted, 3 July 2017.

UPDATING YOUR BRAIN'S SOFTWARE

REMOVING OS "I"

1. Richmond, B.G., "Human evolution: taxonomy and paleobiology". *Journal of Anatomy.* **197** (Pt 1): 19–60, 2000.

2. Ramana Maharshi, in *Wikipedia, The Free Encyclopedia,* Retrieved from https://en.wikipedia.org/w/index.php?title=Ramana_Maharshi &oldid=792739151, 14:55, 28 July 2017.

3. Kapleau, Philip, *The Three Pillars of Zen: Teaching, Practice and Enlightenment*", pp 163 – 195, Anchor Books, Garden City, NY, 1980.

4. Ramana Maharshi, *Talks with Ramana Maharshi: On Realizing Abiding Peace and Happiness,* Oct 23, 1936, p. 188, Inner Directions Publishing, Carlsbad, CA, 2000.

5. Warren, Jeff, "The Neuroscience of Suffering – And Its End", *Psychology Tomorrow*, November 26, 2013.

6. www.merriam-webster.com/dictionary/bit.

7. Koch, et al., "How Much the Eye Tells the Brain", *Cell Current Biology*, Volume 16, Issue 14, p1428–1434, 25 July 2006.

8. Sigman, M. and Dehaene, S., "Brain Mechanisms of Serial and Parallel Processing during Dual-Task Performance", *Journal of Neuroscience, 28 (30) 7585-7598,* 23 July 2008.

SUCCESS

1. Kapleau, Philip, *The Three Pillars of Zen: Teaching, Practice and Enlightenment,* Anchor Press, Garden City, NY, p. 299, 1980.

2. Packer, T., "Remembering meditation teacher Toni Packer (1927 – 2013)". *Lion's Roar.* August 24, 2013.

3. Senzaki, N., Nakagawa, S., Shimano, E., *Namu Dai Bosa: a transmission of Zen Buddhism to America, Nordstrom, Louis, ed.,* Theatre Arts Books, NY, NY, 1976.

4. Mason, P. *The Knack of Meditation: The No-Nonsense Guide to Successful Meditation,* Premanand, Open Sky Press, London, UK, 2013.

   b) *"Who else believes 'no thoughts' is the goal of meditation?"* @ happinessbeyondthought.blogspot.com/2013/11/who-else-believes-no-thoughts-is-goal.html).

5. Wilson, J. et al., "Just Think: The Challenges of the Disengaged Mind", *Science,* Vol. 345, Issue 6192, pp. 75-77, 04 Jul 2014.

6. Charles, F., *History of Philosophy: Descartes to Leibniz,* p. 155, Copleston, Search Press, Kent, England, 1958.

7. Epel, et al., "Wandering Minds and Aging Cells", *Clinical Psychological Science,* 1(1) 75–83, 2013.

8. Killingsworth, M. A., & Gilbert, D. T. "A wandering mind is an un-happy mind", *Science*, 330, 932–932, 2010.

INSTALL A NEW OS MINI-ME

1. Nisargadatta - *I Am That: Talks With Sri Nisargadatta Maharaj, Trans by Maurice Frydman, Ed by Sudhakar Dikshit* Acorn Press, Durham, NC, 1973.

2. Ramana Maharshi, *Upadesa Saram: The Essence of Instruction, The Complete Version in Four Languages Composed by Sri Bhagavan*, Sri Ramanasramam, Tiruvannamalai, India, 2011.

3. Ramana Maharshi, *The Song Celestial*, Sri Ramanasramam, Tiruvannamalai, India, 1995.

4. Andrews-Hannah, et al., "The default network and self-generated thought: component processes, dynamic control, and clinical relevance", *Ann. N.Y. Acad. Sci.*, 1 – 24, New York Academy of Sciences, NY, NY, 2014.

5. Weber, G., *Happiness Beyond Thought: A Practical Guide to Awakening*", iUniverse, Lincoln, NE, 2007.

6. Weber, G., *Dancing Beyond Thought: Bhagavad Gita Verses and Dialogues on Awakening*, CreateSpace Independent Publishing Platform, North Charleston, SC, 2013.

DISCONTINUE SUPPORT FOR THE CONFIRMATION BIAS PROGRAM.

1. Plous, S., *The Psychology of Judgment and Decision Making*, p. 233, McGraw Hill, NY, NY, 1993.

2. Westen, et al. "Neural bases of motivated reasoning: an FMRI study of emotional constraints on partisan political judgment in the 2004 U.S. Presidential election", *Journal of Cognitive Neuroscience*, 18(11): 1947-58, Nov, 2006.

3. Goyal, et al., "Meditation programs for psychological stress and well-being; a systematic review and meta- analysis", *JAMA Internal Med*, 174 (3):357-68, Mar 2014.

4. Lubbers, E., "There is no such thing as the Denver Guardian, despite that Facebook post you saw", *Denver Post*, 05–11-2016.

5. Sydell, Laura, "We Tracked Down a Fake-News Creator in the Suburbs. Here's What We Learned", *NPR, All Tech Considered*, November 23, 2016.

6. Kirby, E. J., "The City Getting Rich on Fake News", *BBC News Magazine*, 5 December, 2016.

7. Oatmeal - theoatmeal.com/comics/believe, May 2, 2017.

8. Associated Press. "George Washington's false teeth not wooden", re-trieved from http://www.nbcnews.com/id/6875436/#.USNzu1ptUow, Jan 27, 2005.

9. Etter, W., "Wooden Teeth Myth", *the Digital Encyclopedia of George Washington*, July 20, 2017.

10. Gehred, K., "Did George Washington's false teeth come from his slaves? A look at the evidence, the responses to that evidence, and the limitations of history", *Washington's Quill*, October 19, 2016.

11. Beschloss, M., "George Washington's Weakness: His Teeth", *NY Times*, April 28, 2014.

UNINSTALL RECIPROCAL ALTRUISM PROGRAM AND UPGRADE TO OPEN SOURCE

1. *Oxford Illustrated American Dictionary* (1998), *Merriam-Webster Collegiate Dictionary* (2000)

2. Liddell, H. G., Scott, R.; Robert Scott *"An Intermediate Greek-English Lexicon: Founded Upon the Seventh Edition of Liddell and Scott's Greek-English Lexicon"*, Benediction Classics. p. 4, 2010,

3. Marien, C., "How homo sapiens became the ultimate invasive species", *Scientific American*, August 2015.

4. Dalai Lama - "Dalai Lama: Helping others is 'wise-selfish' since all are connected", Campbell, Kay, *Twitter* @ www.al.com/living/index.ssf/2013/10/dalai_lama_helping_others_is_w.html, October 09, 2013.

5. Dawkins, Richard, *The Selfish Gene (30th Anniversary ed.),* Oxford University Press, Oxford, UK, 2006.

6. Trivers, R.L., "The evolution of reciprocal altruism", *Quarterly Review of Biology.* **46**: 35–57, 1971.

7. Stevens, Christopher, "Modelling Reciprocal Altruism", *J Philos Sci*, 47 (4): 533-551, 1996.

8. Dalai Lama, HH, *Beyond Religion: Ethics for a Whole World*, 2011, Houghton-Mifflin, NY, NY, 2011.

9. Weber, G., "Upgrading your mental operating system", youtu.be/ EK8pcUt4gio, 2014.

USE MALWARE REMOVAL TOOLS ON THE ATTACHMENTS PROGRAMS

1. "The Four Noble Truths" @ Zen Buddhism: The Source of Zen On the Web, www.zen-buddhism.net/buddhist-principles/four-noble-truths.html, retrieved 2 July 2107.

2. Sharma, Chandradhar, *Indian Philosophy: A Critical Survey*. Barnes & Noble, NY, NY, 1962.

3. Tejomayanandji, Swami, *Shree Sankaracharya's Nirvana Shatakam, commentary by Swami Tejomayanandji,* Central Chinmaya Mission Trust, Mumbai, India, 2001.

4. Shankara, "Nirvana Shatkam - Works of Sankaracharya, Advaita Vedānta and Hindu Sacred Scriptures" @ Sankaracharya.org. 2007-09-22, retrieved 2 July 2014.

5. The Work of Byron Katie - www.thework.com/en

6. The Sedona Method - www.sedona.com

7. Weber, G., "Letting go of your attachments to awaken…why/how/ when" @ happinessbeyondthought.blogspot.com/2014/06/letting-go-of-your-attachments-to.html, 2014.

8. Weber, G., "Surrendering the 'I', letting go of suffering" @ happinessbeyondthought.blogspot.com/2012/05/surrendering-i-letting-go-of-suffering.html, 2012.

9. Weber, G. and Doyle, R., "Letting go of suffering and attachments" @ youtu.be/BVqANXVTLN4, 2016.

UNINSTALL THE "FREE WILL, I'M IN CONTROL" PROGRAM.

1. Harris, S. *Lying*, Four Elephants Press, 2013, Ann Arbor, MI.

2. Harris, Sam, *Free Will*, Free Press, Simon and Schuster, NY, NY, 2012.

3. Eagleman, D., "Who Is In Control?, Episode 3, The Brain With David Eagleman", *PBS*, 10-29-2015.

4. Libet, et al., "Time of Conscious Intention To Act in Relation to Onset of Cerebral Activity: The Unconscious Initiation of a Freely Voluntary Act", *Brain*, 106 (Pt 3):623-42, Sep 1983.

5. Haynes, J., "Decoding and Predicting Intentions", *Ann N Y Acad Sci.* 1224:9-21 Apr. 2011.

6. Fried, l, et al., "Internally Generated Preactivation of Single Neurons in Human Medial Frontal Cortex Predicts Volition", *Neuron*, 69(3):548-62, Feb 10, 2011.

7. Clark, Ronald W., *Einstein: The Life and Times*, p. 422, Harper Collins, NY, NY, 1971.

8. Harris, Sam, *Free Will*, Free Press, NY, NY, 2012.

9. Ramana Maharshi, *Talks With Ramana Maharshi: On Realizing Abiding Peace and Happiness*, p. 186, October 23, 1936, Inner Directions Publishing, Carlsbad, CA, 2000.

10. Farahany, NA, "Neuroscience and behavioral genetics in US criminal law: an empirical analysis", *J Law Biosci.* 2(3): 485–509, Nov 2015.

11. Cowell, A., "After 350 Years, Vatican Says Galileo Was Right: It Moves", NY Times", Oct 31, 1992.

H . D .

I N ' S . . . . .

della Sera, *Sapienza Academics Reject Pope's University* ¦nglish edition), 01-15- 2008.

13. Weber, G., "There's no 'free will'... accept it, attack it, hide it or ignore it?" @ happinessbeyondthought.blogspot.com/2016/09/theres-no-free-willaccept-it-attack-it.html, 2016.

A Powerful Tool For Updating Your Brain's Software – The Ribhu Gita

Introduction

1. Osborne, A. *Ramana Maharshi and the Path of Self Knowledge*, p. 81, Sri Ramanasramam, Tiruvannamali, Tamil Nadu, India, 2002.

2. Ramana Maharshi, *Bhagavan in the Kitchen*, Ramana Smriti Souvenir, 1980.

3. Aiyer, N. R. K., *The Essence of Ribhu Gita - Selection and English Translation*, Sri Ramanasramam, Tiruvannamalai, Tamil Nadu, India, 1984.

4. Ramamoorthy, H., *The Ribhu Gita - First English Translation from the Original Indian Epic Sivarahasya*, Society of Abidance in Truth, Sri Aurobindo Ashram Press, 1995.

5. Deussen, Paul, Bedekar, V.M. (tr.); Palsule (tr.), G.B., *Sixty Upanishads of the Veda*, Motilal Banarsidass Publ., Mumbai, India, 1997.

6. Rao, L. and Sharma, A., *The Ribhu Gita: Sixth Amsa of Sri Siva Rahasyam; The First Complete Edition With English Translation, Transliteration and Original Sanskrit Text.* Sri Ramanasramam, Tiruvannamali, Tamil Nadu, India, 2009.

7. Mason, P., *The Knack of Meditation*, Premanand, Open Sky Press, Hildorf, Germany, 2013.

8. Buckner, R. L., et al., "The Brain's Default Network: Anatomy, Function, and Relevance to Disease", *Annals of the New York Academy of Sciences*. **1124** (1): 1–38, 2008.

9. Andrews-Hanna, J. et al., "The default network and self-generated thought: component processes, dynamic control, and clinical relevance", *Ann. N.Y. Acad. Sci.* 1316, 29–52 CÁ 2014 New York Academy of Sciences, 2014.

10. www.huffingtonpost.com/bruce-davis-phd/healthy-relationships_b_3307916.html.

11. Wilson, T. et al, "Just Think: The Challenges of the Disengaged Mind", *Science*: Vol. 345, Issue 6192, pp. 75-77, 04 Jul 2014.

12. Weber, G., *Dancing Beyond Thought: Bhagavad Gita Verses and Dialogues on Awakening*, p. 26, CreateSpace Independent Publishing Platform, North Charleston, SC, 2013.

ARE MY THOUGHTS USEFUL? HOW DO THEY "BEHAVE"?

1. Dictionary.com and Google

2. "The Brain With David Eagleman", Episode 3", *PBS* @ www.pbs.org/the-brain-with-david-eagleman/episodes/who-is-in-control/, 2014.

3. Sandkhuler, S. and Bhattacharya, J., "Deconstructing Insight: EEG Correlates of Insightful Problem Solving," *PLoS ONE*, Issue 1, e 1459, January 2008.

4. Sheth, B., Sandkhuler, S. and Bhattacharya, J. "Posterior Beta and Anterior Gamma Oscillations Predict Cognitive Insight", *Journal of Cognitive Neuroscience*, 21:7, pp 1269 – 1279, 2008.

JUST HOW UNREAL ARE MY THOUGHTS?

1. Ramana Maharshi, *Talks with Ramana Maharshi: On Realizing Abiding Peace and Happiness*", January 13, 1937, p. 244, Inner Directions Publishing, Carlsbad, CA, 2000.

2. Ramana Maharshi, *Talks with Ramana Maharshi: On Realizing Abiding Peace and Happiness*, February 23, 1937, p. 280, Inner Directions Publishing, Carlsbad, CA, 2000.

3. Gambhiiraananda, Swami, *BhagavadGiiTaa, With the Commentary of Sankaraacaarya*, Advaita Ashrama, p, 297, Calcutta, India, 2003.

WHAT AM I? WHAT IS THE SELF? DO MY THOUGHTS HAVE VALUE?

1. The Zen Studies Society, *Daily Sutras for Chanting and Recitation*, p. 3, New York, New York, 1982.

2. Sutra Translation Committee of the U.S. and Canada, *The Prajna Paramita Heart Sutra*, p. 31, New York, New York, 1995.

3. Weber, G., "Dark Night of the Soul"...who/why/what to do?" @ happinessbeyondthought.blogspot.com/2014/02/dark-night-of-soul-whowhywhat-to-do.html, 2014.

4. Andrews-Hanna, J, et al., "Functional-Anatomic Fractionation of the Brain's Default Network", *Neuron*. 65(4): 550–562, 25 Feb 2010.

5. Weber, G. and Doyle, R, "Shut Up and Chant" @ youtu.be/a4SKQ-fi9568, 2013.

6. Widgery, A. "The principles of Hindu Ethics", *International Journal of Ethics*, Vol. 40, No. 2, pages 234-237. 1930.

7. Gambhiiraananda, Swami, *BhagavadGiiTaa, With the Commentary of Sankaraacaarya*, Advaita Ashrama, pp, 584 - 6, Calcutta, India, 2003.

HOW DO BONDAGE, SIN AND SAMSARA ARISE?

1. Monier-Williams, M., *A Sanskrit-English Dictionary*, p. 835, Motilal Banarsidass Publishers Pvt. Ltd, Delhi, India, 2005.

2. Gambhiiraananda, Swami, *BhagavadGiiTaa, With the Commentary of Sankaraacaarya*, Advaita Ashrama, pp, 735 - 6, Calcutta, India, 2003.

3. Longchengpa, *You Are the Eyes of the World*, translated by M. Peterson and K. Lipman", Snow Lion, Boulder, CO, US, 2000.

WHERE DOES THE CONCEPT OF A "BODY" COME FROM?

1. Ball, P., *The Elements: A Very Short Introduction*. Very Short Introductions. Oxford University Press, Oxford, UK. p. 33, 2004.

2. Ramana Maharshi, *Upadesa Saram: The Complete Version in Four Languages Composed by Sri Bhagavan*, Sri Ramanasramam, Tiruvannamalai, India, 2011.

WHERE DOES THE FEELING OF A "KNOT" IN OUR HEART COME FROM?

1. Ramana Maharshi, *Spiritual Instruction of Bhagavan Sri Ramana Maharshi*, Sri Ramanasramam, Tiruvannamalai, S. India, 1974.

WHERE DOES THE SENSE OF DIFFERENT BODIES COME FROM?

1. Weber, G. "How 'consciousness' creates matter...the God particle", happinessbeyondthought.blogspot.com/2013/02/how-consciousness-creates-matterthe-god.html, 2013.

2. Tummer, Lia, *Rudolf Steiner and Anthroposophy for Beginners*, Writers and Readers Publishing, pp. 64-69, 91, 2001.

WHERE DOES THE SENSE OF "REAL" AND "UNREAL" ORIGINATE?

1. Weber, G., "What is really 'real'? What does 'nothing is real' mean?" at happinessbeyondthought.blogspot.com/2013/07/what-is-really-real-what-does-nothing.html.

2. Andrews-Hannah, J, et al., "Functional-Anatomic Fractionation of the Brain's Default Network", *Neuron*. 65(4): 550–562, 25 Feb 2010.

3. Weber, G., "Three Neural Networks Dancing...'blah, blah', tasking and control" @ happinessbeyondthought.blogspot.com/2014/07/three-neural-networks-dancing-blah-blah.html, 2014.

4. Norretranders, Tor, "Inside Out: The Epistemology of Everything" pp. 267-270 in *This Will Change Everything: Ideas That Will Shape The Future*, Brockman, John, Harper-Collins, NY, NY, 2009.

5. Weber, G., "Do your mystical experiences fit w/quantum physics? neuroscience?" @ happinessbeyondthought.blogspot.com/2012/12/do-your-mystical-experiences-like.html, 2012.

WHERE DOES THE IDEA THAT THERE IS A WORLD COME FROM?

1. Ball, P. *The Elements: A Very Short Introduction*. Very Short Introductions. Oxford University Press, Oxford, UK. p. 33, 2004.

WHERE DO OUR BIASES AND MISCONCEPTIONS COME FROM?

1. Weber, G., "How neuroscience, psychological studies and our poor memories change the law..." @ happinessbeyondthought.blogspot. com/2012/12/how-neuroscience-psychological-studies.html, 2012.

WHERE DOES THE IDEA THAT WE ARE A SEPARATE INDIVIDUAL COME FROM?

1. Freeman, W.H. *The Current Mass Extinction* @ /www.pbs.org/wgbh/ evolution/library/03/2/l_032_04.html, 2001.

2. Biggs, Alton et al. *"Biology: The Dynamics of Life"*, by Merrill Publishing, Princeton, NC, 1991.

WHERE DOES OUR CONCEPT OF A "MIND" COME FROM?

1. Ramana Maharshi, *Upadesa Saram: The Complete Version in Four Languages Composed by Sri Bhagavan*, Sri Ramanasramam, Tiruvannamalai, India, pp 116 –118, 2011.

WHY DO WE BELIEVE WE ARE DIFFERENT FROM EVERYTHING ELSE?

1. Andrews-Hannah, J, et al., "Functional-Anatomic Fractionation of the Brain's Default Network", *Neuron.* 65(4): 550–562, 25 Feb 2010.

WHERE DO OUR SORROWS COME FROM?

1. Koch, et al., "How Much the Eye Tells the Brain", *Cell Current Biology*, Volume 16, Issue 14, p1428–1434, 25 July 2006.

2. Sigman, M and Dehaene, S, "Brain Mechanisms of Serial and Parallel Processing during Dual-Task Performance", *Journal of Neuroscience*, 28 (30) 7585-7598, 23 July 2008.

3. Weber, Gary, *Right-sizing your 'I', understanding confirmation bias…new studies* @ happinessbeyondthought.blogspot.com/2017/05/right-sizing-your-i-understanding.html, 2017.

WHAT IS THE GREAT MISTAKE THAT THE "I" MAKES?

1. Weber, Gary, *Right-sizing your 'I', understanding confirmation bias… new studies,* @ happinessbeyondthought.blogspot.com/2017/05/right-sizing-your-i-understanding.html, 2017.

2. Eagleman, David, "Are our lives controlled by our unconscious brain*?*" @ www.pbs.org/the-brain-with-david-eagleman/episodes/who-is-in-control/, *PBS*, 2015.

WHERE DOES THE IDEA OF "DEATH" COME FROM?

1. Gambhiiraananda, Swami, *BhagavadGiiTaa, With the Commentary of Sankaraacaarya*, Advaita Ashrama, pp. 75 - 77, Calcutta, India, 2003.

JUST HOW SERIOUS IS THIS MISTAKEN BELIEF THAT "I AM THIS BODY"?

1. Liddell, H. G. and Scott, R.; *A Greek–English Lexicon* at the Perseus Project, Tufts University, Medford, MA.

2. Pagels, E. *The Gnostic Gospels*. Vintage Books: New York, 1989. p. 123.

DOES THE "I AM THIS BODY" BELIEF CAUSE ALL OF MY "FAULTS"?

1. Frawley, David, *Yoga and Ayurveda: Self-Healing and Self-Realization*, Lotus Press, Twin Lakes, WI, (1999).

2. Monier-Williams, M., *A Sanskrit English Dictionary*, p. 498, Motilal Banarsidass Publishers, Delhi, India, (2002).

3. Nagamma, Suri, *Letters from Sri Ramanasramam*, 4 April 1947, (103) Human Effort, Sri Ramanasramam, Tiruvannamalai, India, (2006).

4. Ramana Maharshi, *Upadesa Saram: The Complete Version in Four Language composed by Sri Bhagavan*, pp. 118-120, Sri Ramanasramam, Tiruvannamalai, India (2011).

IF I'M NOT THIS BODY, THEN WHAT AM I?

1. Gambhiiraananda, Swami, *BhagavadGiiTaa, With the Commentary of Sankaraacaarya*, Advaita Ashrama, pp. 412 - 413, Calcutta, India, 2003.

2. Gambhiiraananda, Swami, *BhagavadGiiTaa, With the Commentary of Sankaraacaarya*, Advaita Ashrama, pp. 557 - 558, Calcutta, India, 2003.

3. Gambhiiraananda, Swami, *BhagavadGiiTaa, With the Commentary of Sankaraacaarya*, Advaita Ashrama, pp. 72 - 73, Calcutta, India, 2003.

WHAT IS THE ULTIMATE TEACHER?

1. Ramana Maharshi, *Talks with Ramana Maharshi: On Realizing Abiding Peace and Happiness*, Inner Directions Publishing, Carlsbad, CA, (2000), p. 188, October 23, 1936.

2. Ford, James Ishmael, *Zen Master Who? A Guide to the People and Stories of Zen*, (2006), Wisdom Publications, pp. 159–62, Somerville, MA.

WHAT IS THE TRANSCENDENTAL ILLUMINATING LIGHT?

1. Staal, Frits (June 1986). "The sound of religion". *Numen*. **33**(Fasc. 1): 33–64.

2. Rahman, M. M. (1 January 2005). *Encyclopaedia of Historiography*. Anmol Publications Pvt. Limited, New Delhi, India.

3. Shults, Brett (May 2014), "On the Buddha's Use of Some Brahmanical Motifs in Pali Texts". *Journal of the Oxford Centre for Buddhist Studies*. **6**: 119. Wolfson College, Linton Road, Oxford, England.

4. Rinehart, Robin, (1 January 2004), *Contemporary Hinduism: Ritual, Culture, and Practice*. ABC-CLIO.

HOW DOES ONE MOVE BEYOND THE EVERYDAY DANCE OF ENERGY?

1. Gambhiiraananda, Swami, *BhagavadGiiTaa, With the Commentary of Sankaraacaarya*, Advaita Ashrama, pp. 587 - 588, Calcutta, India, 2003.

2. Godman, David, *Living By The Words of Bhagavan*, Annamalai Swami Ashram, Palakottu, Sri Ramanasramam P.O., Tiruvannamalai 606603, India, 1994.

CAN WE REACH A PERMANENT, PEACEFUL STATE?

1. Ramana Maharshi, *Upadesa Saram: The Complete Version in Four Language composed by Sri Bhagavan*, pp 128, 129, Sri Ramanasramam, Tiruvannamalai, India (2011).

DOES THIS STATE EXTEND EVERYWHERE AND IS IT STABLE?

1. Gambhiiraananda, Swami, *BhagavadGiiTaa, With the Commentary of Sankaraacaarya*, Advaita Ashrama, pp. 557 - 558, Calcutta, India, 2003.

KNOWLEDGE OF THE SELF

1. Victor Sōgen Hori *Zen sand: the book of capping phrases for kōan practice.* University of Hawai'i Press, Honolulu, HI (2003).

2. Sōiku Shigematsu *A Zen Forest: Sayings of the Masters.* Compiled and translated, with an introduction. John Weatherhill, Inc., NY, NY (1981).

3. Kapleau, Philip, *The Three Pillars of Zen: Teaching, Practice and Enlightenment,* pp. 163 – 195, Anchor Books, NY, NY (1989).

4. Weber, Gary, https://soundcloud.com/gary_weber.

5. Weber, Gary, https://www.youtube.com/channel/UCMSnyxnteEx7IOPIFkfh3og.

HOW DOES THE SOFTWARE UPDATE PROCESS UNFOLD IN THE REAL WORLD?

1. Csikszentmihalyi, M., *"Flow: The Psychology of Optimal Experience",* Harper Collins, NY, NY, 1990.

2. Weber, G., "How 'consciousness' creates matter...the God particle" @ happinessbeyondthought.blogspot.com/2013/02/how-consciousness-creates-matterthe-god.html, 2013.

3. Weber, G., *"Traumatic memories feel true, but are always changing"* @happinessbeyondthought.blogspot.com/2012/01/traumatic-memories-feel-true-but-are.html, 2012.

4. Weber, G., "How do i deal with anger? i can't meditate it away" @ happinessbeyondthought.blogspot.com/2012/09/how-do-i-deal-with-anger-i-cant.html, 2012.

5. Weber, G., "Do drugs, sex, competition and meditation use the same "pleasure" system" @ happinessbeyondthought.blogspot.com/2013/11/do-drugs-sex-competition-and-meditation.html, (2013).

6. Weber, G., "'Blah-blah'- understanding its contents and effects...recent research" @ happinessbeyondthought.blogspot.com/2014/10/blah-blah-understanding-its-content-and.html, 2014.

7. Weber, G., "Why do we sleep? Evolutionary mistake? 'Catch up' napping..." @ happinessbeyondthought.blogspot.com/2013/11/why-do-we-sleep-evolutionary-mistake.html, 2013.

THE GREATEST RESISTANCE TO CHANGING THE SOFTWARE - "FREE WILL"

1. Einstein, A., *The Life and Times*, Clark, R. W., p. 422, Avon Books, Harper Collins, NY, NY, 2001.

2. Ramana Maharshi, *Day by Day with Bhagavan*, p. 211, Mudaliar, A. Devaraja, 5th Edition, Sri Ramanasramam, Tiruvannamalai, Tamil Nadu, India, 2002.

"THERE'S NO FREE WILL...ACCEPT IT, ATTACK IT, HIDE IT OR IGNORE IT?"

1. Bassui, Tokushoo, "Dharma Talk On One Mind", in *Three Pillars of Zen: Teaching, Practice and Enlightenment*, Kapleau, Philip, pp. 164-172, Anchor Books, Garden City, NY, 1980.

2. Harris, Sam, *Waking Up: A Guide to Spirituality Without Religion*, Simon & Schuster, NY, NY, 2014.

3. Weber, G., "How 'consciousness' creates matter...the God particle" @ happinessbeyondthought.blogspot.com/2013/02/how-consciousness-creates-matterthe-god.html, 2013.

4. Weber, G., and Doyle, R., "Are 'we' just outdated, buggy programs?" @ youtu.be/dnfNn4I6Zbg, 2016.

"ARE OUR LIVES CONTROLLED BY OUR UNCONSCIOUS BRAIN?"

1. Weber, G., "Feeling your way to nondual awakening" @ happinessbeyondthought.blogspot.com/2015/04/feeling-your-way-to-nondual-awakening.html, 2015.

"OUR "CHOICES" ARE RANDOM?...NEW RESEARCH"

1. Wright, Robert, *The Moral Animal: Why We Are The Way We Are: The New Science of Evolutionary Psychology*, Vintage Books, NY, NY, 1995.

2. Weber, G., and Doyle, R., "Predestination, control, free will and the illusion of time" @ youtu.be/kYkf7L0oY84, 2013.

"THE IMPOSSIBILITY OF "FREE WILL"...SCIENTIFICALLY AND LOGICALLY"

1. Weber, G., "Surrendering the 'I', letting go of suffering" @ happinessbeyondthought.blogspot.com/2012/05/surrendering-i-letting-go-of-suffering.html, 2012.

2. Ramana Maharshi, *Maharshi's Gospel,* pp. 7-8, Venkataraman, T.N., Sri Ramanasramam, Tiruvannamalai, Tamil Nadu, India, 2002.

"I GET "NO FREE WILL" INTELLECTUALLY, BUT CAN'T MAKE IT "REAL"... WHAT TO DO?"

1. Weber, G., "You say 'we have no free will', and "we're not in control"...Is that experience, science or philosophy?" @ happinessbeyondthought.blogspot. com/2012/10/you-say-we-have-no-free-will-and-were.html, 2012.

2. Weber, G., "Is everything predetermined or just the big stuff?" @ happinessbeyondthought.blogspot.com/2012/02/is-everything-pre-determined-or-just-big.html, 2012.

"YOU SAY "WE HAVE NO FREE WILL" AND "WE'RE NOT IN CONTROL"... IS THAT EXPERIENCE, SCIENCE, OR PHILOSOPHY?"

1. Bar-Yam, Yaneer, "General Features of Complex Systems" (PDF). *Encyclopedia of Life Support Systems*. EOLSS UNESCO Publishers, Oxford, UK, 2002. Retrieved 16 September 2014.

2. Libet, et al., "Time of Conscious Intention To Act in Relation to Onset of Cerebral Activity: The Unconscious Initiation of a Freely Voluntary Act", *Brain*, 106 (Pt 3):623-42, Sep 1983.

3. Crick, F., "Introduction", *The Astonishing Hypothesis: The Scientific Search for Soul*, Touchstone, Simon and Schuster, p. 3, NY, NY, (1994).

"FREE WILL VERSUS NEUROSCIENCE: BELIEF VS SCIENCE"

1. Galileo Galilei. (2017, July 25). In *Wikipedia, The Free Encyclopedia*. Retrieved 21:33, August 1, 2017 from https://en.wikipedia.org/w/in-dex.php?title=Galileo_Galilei&oldid=792234592.

Bibliography

Clark, Ronald W., *Einstein: The Life and Times*, p. 422, Harper Collins, NY, NY, 1971.

Gambhiiraananda, Swami, *BhagavadGiiTaa, With the Commentary of Sankaraacaarya*, Advaita Ashrama, p, 297, Calcutta, India, 2003.

Godman, David, *Living By The Words of Bhagavan*, Annamalai Swami Ashram, Palakottu, Sri Ramanasramam P.O., Tiruvannamalai 606603, India, 1994.

Harris, Sam, *Free Will*, Free Press, NY, NY, 2012.

Harris, Sam, *Waking Up: A Guide to Spirituality Without Religion,* Simon & Schuster, NY, NY, 2014.

Kapleau, Philip, *The Three Pillars of Zen: Teaching, Practice and Enlightenment"*, Anchor Books, Garden City, NY, 1980.

Nisargadatta - *I Am That: Talks With Sri Nisargadatta Maharaj, Trans by Maurice Frydman, Ed by Sudhakar Dikshit* Acorn Press, Durham, NC, 1973.

Osborne, A. *Ramana Maharshi and the Path of Self Knowledge*, p. 81, Sri Ramanasramam, Tiruvannamali, Tamil Nadu, India, 2002.

Ramamoorthy, H., *The Ribhu Gita - First English Translation from the Original Indian Epic Sivarahasya*, Society of Abidance in Truth, Sri Aurobindo Ashram Press, 1995.

Ramana Maharshi, *Spiritual Instruction of Bhagavan Sri Ramana Maharshi*, Sri Ramanasramam, Tiruvannamalai, S. India, 1974.

Ramana Maharshi, *Talks with Ramana Maharshi: On Realizing Abiding Peace and Happiness*, Inner Directions Publishing, Carlsbad, CA, 2000.

Ramana Maharshi, *The Song Celestial*, Sri Ramanasramam, Tiruvannamalai, India, 1995.

Ramana Maharshi, *Upadesa Saram: The Essence of Instruction, The Complete Version in Four Languages Composed by Sri Bhagavan*, Sri Ramanasramam, Tiruvannamalai, India, 2011.

Rao, L. and Sharma, A., *The Ribhu Gita: Sixth Amsa of Sri Siva Rahasyam; The First Complete Edition With English Translation, Transliteration and Original Sanskrit Text*. Sri Ramanasramam, Tiruvannamali, Tamil Nadu, India, 2009.

Tejomayanandji, Swami, *Shree Sankaracharya's Nirvana Shatakam*, commentary by Swami Tejomayanandji, Central Chinmaya Mission Trust, Mumbai, India, 2001.

Weber, G., *Dancing Beyond Thought: Bhagavad Gita Verses and Dialogues on Awakening*, CreateSpace Independent Publishing Platform, North Charleston, SC, 2013.

Weber, G., *Happiness Beyond Thought: A Practical Guide to Awakening"*, iUniverse, Lincoln, NE, 2007.

Wright, R., *The Moral Animal; Why We Are the Way We Are: The New Science of Evolutionary Psychology*, Vintage Books, NY, NY, 1995.

APPENDIX: DEVANAGARI SANSKRIT
FOR THE RIBHU GITA VERSES

Are my thoughts useful? How do they "behave"?

चित्तं	एव	महा	दोषं	चित्तं	एव	हि	बालकः
cittam	eva	mahaa	doshaM	cittam	eva	hi	baalakaH

चित्तं	एव	महा	आत्म	अयं	चित्तं	एव	महा	अनसत
cittam	eva	maha	atma	ayaM	cittam	eva	maha	anasat

Just how unreal are my thoughts?

चित्तं	एव	हि	मिथ्य	आत्म	चित्तं	शश	विशनवत
cittam	eva	hi	mithya	atma	cittaM	shasha	vishanavat

चित्तं	नास्ति	सदा	सत्यं	चित्तं	वन्ध्या	कुमारवत
cittam	naasti	sadaa	satyaM	cittaM	vandhyaa	kumaaravat

What am I? What is the Self? Do my thoughts have value?

चित्तं	शून्यं	न	सन्देहः	ब्रह्म	एव	सकलं	जगत्
cittam	shuunyaM	na	sandehaH	brahma	eva	sakalaM	jagat

अहं	एव	हि	चैतन्यं	अहं	एव	हि	निर्	गुणं
aham	eva	hi	caitanyaM	aham	eva	hi	nir	gunam

How do bondage, sin and samsara arise?

मन	एव	हि	संसारं	मन	एव	हि	मण्डलं
mana	eva	hi	saMsaaraM	mana	eva	hi	mandalam

मन	एव	हि	बन्धत्वं	मन	एव	हि	पातकम्
mana	eva	hi	bandhatvaM	mana	eva	hi	paatakam

Where does the concept of a "body" come from?

मन	एव	महद्	दुखं	मन	एव	शरीरकं
mana	eva	mahad	duhkhaM	mana	eva	shariirakam

मन	एव	प्रपञ्चाख्यं	मन	एव	कलेबरं
mana	eva	prapancaakhyaM	mana	eva	kalebaram

Where does the feeling of a "knot" in our heart come from?

देहे	अहं	इति	सङ्कल्पः	हृदय	ग्रन्थिर	ईरितः
dehe	aham	iti	sankalpaH	hrdydaya	granthir	iritaH

काल	त्रयेपि	तन्न	अस्ति	सर्वं	ब्रह्म	एति	केवलं
kaala	trayepi	tanna	asti	sarvam	brahma	eti	kevalam

Where does the sense of different bodies come from?

देह	त्रये	अपि	भावं	यत्	तद्	देह	ज्ञानं	उच्यते
dehe	tri	epi	bhaavam	yat	tad	deha	jnanam	ucyate

काल	त्रयेपि	तन्न	अस्ति	सर्वं	ब्रह्म	एति	केवलं
kaala	trayepi	tanna	asti	sarvam	brahma	eti	kevalam

Where does the sense of "real" and "unreal" originate?

देहे	अहं	इति	यद्	भावं	सद	असद	भावं	एव	च
dehe	aham	iti	yad	bhaavam	sad	asad	bhaavam	eva	ca

काल	त्रयेपि	तन्न	अस्ति	सर्वं	ब्रह्म	एति	केवलं
kaala	trayepi	tanna	asti	sarvam	brahma	eti	kevalam

Where does the idea that there is a world come from?

देहे	अहं	इति	सङ्कल्पः	तत्	प्रपन्चामि	होच्यते
dehe	aham	iti	sankalpaH	tat	prapancaami	hocyate

काल	त्रयेपि	तन्न	अस्ति	सर्वं	ब्रह्म	एति	केवलं
kaala	trayepi	tanna	asti	sarvam	brahma	eti	kevalam

What is the fundamental source of our misunderstandings?

देहे	अहं	इति	सङ्कल्पः	तत्	एव	अज्ञानं	उच्यते
dehe	aham	iti	sankalpaH	tat	eva	ajnanam	ucyate

काल	त्रयेपि	तन्न	अस्ति	सर्व	ब्रह्म	एति	केवलं
kaala	trayepi	tanna	asti	sarvam	brahma	eti	kevalam

Where do our biases and misconceptions come from?

देहे	अहं	इति	या	बुद्धिः	मलिना	वसन्	उच्यते
dehe	aham	iti	yaa	buddhiH	malinaa	vaasan	ucyate

काल	त्रयेपि	तन्न	अस्ति	सर्व	ब्रह्म	एति	केवलं
kaala	trayepi	tanna	asti	sarvam	brahma	eti	kevalam

Where does the idea that we are a separate individual come from?

देहे	अहं	इति	या	बुद्धिः	सत्यं	जीवः	स	एव	सः
dehe	aham	iti	yaa	buddhiH	satyaM	jivaH	sa	eva	saH

काल	त्रयेपि	तन्न	अस्ति	सर्व	ब्रह्म	एति	केवलं
kaala	trayepi	tanna	asti	sarvam	brahma	eti	kevalam

How does this belief that we are these bodies, manifest in our lives?

देहे	अहं	इति	सङ्कल्पः	महा	अनरकं	ईरितम्
dehe	aham	iti	sankalpaH	maha	anarakam	iiritam

काल	त्रयेपि	तन्न	अस्ति	सर्वं	ब्रह्म	एति	केवलं
kaala	trayepi	tanna	asti	sarvam	brahma	eti	kevalam

Where does our concept of a "mind" come from?

देहे	अहं	इति	या	बुद्धिः	मन	एविति	निश्चितम्
dehe	aham	iti	yaa	buddhiH	mana	eviti	nishcitam

काल	त्रयेपि	तन्न	अस्ति	सर्वं	ब्रह्म	एति	केवलं
kaala	trayepi	tanna	asti	sarvam	brahma	eti	kevalam

Why do we believe we are different from everything else?

देहे	अहं	इति	या	बुद्धिः	परिच्छिन्नं	इतीर्यते
dehe	aham	iti	yaa	buddhiH	paricchinnam	itiiryate

काल	त्रयेपि	तन्न	अस्ति	सर्वं	ब्रह्म	एति	केवलं
kaala	trayepi	tanna	asti	sarvam	brahma	eti	kevalam

Where do our sorrows come from?

देहे	अहं	इति	यद्	ज्ञानं	सर्वं	शोक	इतीरितम्
dehe	aham	iti	yad	jnaanaM	sarvaM	shoka	itiiritam

काल	त्रयेपि	तन्न	अस्ति	सर्वं	ब्रह्म	एति	केवलं
kaala	trayepi	tanna	asti	sarvam	brahma	eti	kevalam

What is the great mistake that the "I" makes?

देहे	अहं	इति	यद्	ज्ञानं	संस्पर्शमिति	कथ्यते
dehe	aham	iti	yad	jnaanaM	saMsparshamiti	kathyate

काल	त्रयेपि	तन्न	अस्ति	सर्वं	ब्रह्म	एति	केवलं
kaala	trayepi	tanna	asti	sarvam	brahma	eti	kevalam

Where does the idea of "death" come from?

देहे	अहं	इति	या	बुद्धिः	तदेव	मरणं	स्मृतम्
dehe	aham	iti	yaa	buddhiH	tadeva	maranaM	smrtam

काल	त्रयेपि	तन्न	अस्ति	सर्वं	ब्रह्म	एति	केवलं
kaala	trayepi	tanna	asti	sarvam	brahma	eti	kevalam

What is wrong with the idea that "I am this body"?

देहे	अहं	इति	या	बुद्धिः	तदेव	अशोभनं	स्मृतम्
dehe	aham	iti	yaa	buddhiH	tadeva	ashobhanaM	smrtam

काल	त्रयेपि	तन्न	अस्ति	सर्वं	ब्रह्म	एति	केवलं
kaala	trayepi	tanna	asti	sarvam	brahma	eti	kevalam

Just how serious is this mistaken belief that "I am this body"?

देहे	अहं	इति	या	बुद्धिः	महा	अपापमिति	स्मृतम्
dehe	aham	iti	yaa	buddhiH	maha	apaapamiti	smrtam

काल	त्रयेपि	तन्न	अस्ति	सर्वं	ब्रह्म	एति	केवलं
kaala	trayepi	tanna	asti	sarvam	brahma	eti	kevalam

Why is this concept so overwhelming?

देहे	अहं	इति	या	बुद्धिः	तुष्ठा	सैव	हि	चोच्यते
dehe	aham	iti	yaa	buddhiH	tushthaa	saiva	hi	cocyate

काल	त्रयेपि	तन्न	अस्ति	सर्वं	ब्रह्म	एति	केवलं
kaala	trayepi	tanna	asti	sarvam	brahma	eti	kevalam

Does the "I am this body" belief cause all of my "faults"?

देहे	अहं	इति	सङ्कल्पः	सर्व	दोषं	इति	स्मृतम्
dehe	aham	iti	sankalpaH	sarva	dosham	iti	smrtam

काल	त्रयेपि	तन्न	अस्ति	सर्वं	ब्रह्म	एति	केवलं
kaala	trayepi	tanna	asti	sarvam	brahma	eti	kevalam

What is my nature?

अहं	एव	हि	गुप्त	आत्मा	अहं	एव	निरन्तरं
aham	eva	hi	gupta	atmaa	aham	eva	nirantaram

आनन्दं	परमं	मानं	इदं	दृश्यं	न	किञ्चन
aanandaM	paramaM	maanam	idaM	dRshyaM	na	kincana

What is the ultimate teacher?

अहं	एव	परं	ब्रह्म	अहं	एव	गुरोर्	गुरुः
aham	eva	paraM	brahma	aham	eva	guror	guruH

आनन्दं	परमं	मानं	इदं	दृश्यं	न	किञ्चन
aanandaM	paramaM	maanam	idaM	dRshyaM	na	kincana

What is the ultimate happiness?

अहं	एव	अखिला	आधार	अहं	एव	सुखात	सुखं
aham	eva	akhilaa	adhaara	aham	eva	sukhaat	sukham

आनन्दं	परमं	मानं	इदं	दृश्यं	न	किञ्चन
aanandaM	paramaM	maanam	idaM	dRshyaM	na	kincana

What is the transcendental illuminating light?

अहं	एव	परं	ज्योतिः	अहं	एव	अखिला	आत्मकः
aham	eva	paraM	jyotiH	aham	eva	akhilaa	aatmakaH

आनन्दं	परमं	मानं	इदं	दृश्यं	न	किञ्चन
aanandaM	paramaM	maanam	idaM	dRshyaM	na	kincana

How does one move beyond the everyday dance of energy?

अहं	एव	हि	तृप्त	आत्मा	अहं	एव	हि	निर्	गुणः
aham	eva	hi	tRpta	atmaa	aham	eva	hi	nir	gunaH

आनन्दं	परमं	मानं	इदं	दृश्यं	न	किञ्चन
aanandaM	paramaM	maanam	idaM	dRshyaM	na	kincana

Can we ever fill that "lack", that "incompleteness" that we feel?

अहं	एव	हि	पूर्ण	आत्मा	अहं	एव	पुरातनः
aham	eva	hi	puurna	atmaa	aham	eva	puraatanaH

आनन्दं	परमं	मानं	इदं	दृश्यं	न	किञ्चन
aanandaM	paramaM	maanam	idaM	dRshyaM	na	kincana

Can we reach a permanent, peaceful state?

अहं	एव	हि	शान्त	आत्मा	अहं	एव	हि	शाश्वतः
aham	eva	hi	shaanta	atmaa	aham	eva	hi	shaashvataH

आनन्दं	परमं	मानं	इदं	दृश्यं	न	किञ्चन
aanandaM	paramaM	maanam	idaM	dRshyaM	na	kincana

Does this state extend everywhere and is it stable?

अहं	एव	हि	सर्वत्र	अहं	एव	हि	सुस्थिरः
aham	eva	hi	sarvatra	aham	eva	hi	susthiraH

आनन्दं	परमं	मानं	इदं	दृश्यं	न	किञ्चन
aanandaM	paramaM	maanam	idaM	dRshyaM	na	kincana

Knowledge of the Self

आत्मा	ज्ञानं	परं	शास्त्रं	आत्मा	ज्ञानं	अनूपमं
aatma	jnaanaM	paraM	shaastraM	aatma	jnaanam	anuupamaM

आत्मा	ज्ञानं	परो	योग	आत्मा	ज्ञानं	परा	गतिः
aatma	jnaanaM	paro	yoga	atma	jnaanaM	paraa	gatiH

आत्मा	ज्ञानं	चित्तान	अशः	आत्मा	ज्ञानं	विमुक्तिदम्
aatma	jnaanaM	cittana	ashaH	aatma	jnanaM	vimuktidaM

आत्मा	ज्ञानं	भयान	आशं	आत्मा	ज्ञानं	सुख	अवहम्
aatma	jnaanaM	bhyana	ashaM	aatma	jnaanaM	sukha	avaham

Printed in Great Britain
by Amazon

68010500R00132